How Free Is Free?

The Nathan I. Huggins Lectures

Leon F. Litwack

How Free Is
FREE?

The Long Death
of Jim Crow

HARVARD UNIVERSITY PRESS

Cambridge, Massachusetts, and London, England   2009

Library of Congress Cataloging-in-Publication Data

Litwack, Leon F.

How free is free? : the long death of Jim Crow / Leon F. Litwack

p.   cm. — (The Nathan I. Huggins lectures)

Includes bibliographical references and index.

ISBN 978-0-674-03152-4 (alk. paper)

1. African Americans — Civil rights — Southern States — History.

2. African Americans — Segregation — Southern States — History.

3. African Americans — Southern States — Social conditions.

4. Liberty — Social aspects — Southern States — History.

5. Racism — Southern States — History.   6. Southern States — Race

relations.   I. Title.

E185.61.L593 2009

323.1196'073075 — dc22   2008036468

For Kenneth M. Stampp
mentor and friend

Contents

How Free Is Free?

1 | High Water Everywhere

> They meet with darkness in the daytime. And they
> grope at noonday as in the night.
> —Book of Job, 5:14

> You got to fight to make it [freedom] mean some-
> thing. All it mean is you got a long row to hoe and
> ain't got no plow. Ain't got no seed. Ain't got no mule.
> What good is freedom if you can't do nothing with it?
> —Solly Two Kings, in August Wilson's
> *Gem of the Ocean*

SHORTLY AFTER the Civil War, Oliver Howard, head of the Freedmen's Bureau, a government agency designed to oversee the transition from slavery to freedom, came to Edisto Island, off the coast of South Carolina. The newly freed slaves who lived and worked there knew why he was coming: to order them to surrender to the original owners the lands they had been working as their own after their masters fled during the war. The church in which he met them was jammed with sad and angry blacks who were in no mood to cooperate. Suddenly an old woman began to sing, "Nobody knows the trouble I feel/Nobody knows but Jesus," and the entire audience of some two thousand joined her. Whether it was the song, the look of dismay on the faces before him, or the shouts of "No, no!" that greeted his words, Howard was so flustered that he could barely finish his speech. But he managed to communicate the position of the federal government. He told them to lay aside any bitter feelings they harbored for their former masters and to contract to work for those same masters. If the freedmen found Howard's advice incomprehensible, that was because they understood him all too clearly. A voice from the gallery rang out, "Why, General Howard, why do you take away our lands? You take them from us who are true, always true to the Government! You give them to our all-time enemies! That is not right!"[1] His outburst captured the ultimate irony of this moment. The only serious discussion about compensation after emancipation was not about reparations for freed slaves for centuries of unpaid labor; it was about compensating slaveholders for the loss (confiscation) of their human property.

In July 1966, nearly a century after the Edisto meeting, Martin Luther King Jr. faced a black audience in Chicago. He had come to Chicago to address the violence of poverty, to battle ghetto conditions, and to decry the slumlords and politicians who perpetuated them. He realized by now that segregation was only part of an elaborate system of racial inequality in housing, jobs, income, and education, and he knew that this was not strictly a Southern phenomenon. "If we can break the system in Chicago," King believed, "it can be broken anywhere in the country."[2] But Chicago proved to be a frustrating experience; King and his coworkers came up against a structure that was stronger, more difficult to define, and more damaging in its human costs than any-thing they had confronted in the South. The old tactics of nonviolence, street marches, and mass rallies no longer achieved the desired results. In Chicago, the goal of economic justice proved more elusive, the barriers more formidable. King failed to achieve his objectives there, and when he tried to address a community meet-ing, he encountered for the first time a hostile black au-dience, many of them young, some of whom jeered as he started to speak. With "an ugly feeling," he returned home that night wondering, "Why would they boo one so close to them?" Reflecting on this encounter, he thought he understood.

> For twelve years I, and others like me, had held out radiant promises of progress. I had preached to them about my dream. I had lectured to them about the not too distant day when they would have freedom, "all, here and now." I had urged them to have faith in America and in white society. Their hopes had soared. They were now booing because they felt we were un-able to deliver on our promises. They were booing because we had urged them to have faith in people who had too often proved to be unfaithful. They were now hostile because they were watching the dream that they had so readily accepted turn into a frustrating nightmare.[3]

If nothing else, as King confessed to several journalists, Chicago nationalized the Civil Rights Movement and confirmed for him the endemic, intractable, infinitely varied and resourceful racism of white America.

For more than a century, black Southerners learned to live with betrayed expectations, with diminishing prospects and aspirations. In the 1860s, and a century later in the 1960s, two major struggles, two major civil conflicts were fought over the meaning of freedom in America: over the enslavement of black people and over the legally sanctioned repression of their descendants, over the bonds of slavery and the bonds of segregation and economic strangulation. How free is free? In the lives of black men and women who had known only enslavement, the answer was not at all clear. "I used to think if I could be free I should be the happiest of anybody in the world," a young Mississippi woman recalled. "But when my master come to me, and says—'Lizzie, you is free!' it seems like I was in a kind of daze. And when I would wake up in the morning I would think to myself, Is I free? Hasn't I got to get up before daylight and go into the field to work?"[4]

In the 1860s and in the 1960s, major efforts were undertaken to restructure race relations. In both decades, the United States government made legislative, executive, and judicial commitments to black freedom and civil rights that would in time be compromised, deferred, and undone. And in the late nineteenth century, at the height of the Jim Crow era, and in the late twentieth century, in the aftermath of the Civil Rights Movement, new struggles were waged over problems unresolved by the first and second Reconstructions, struggles over the persistence of racism in a nation that remained separate and unequal, despite court decisions and legislation, despite agitation, marches, and confrontations.

For black Southerners, the period of the late nineteenth and early twentieth centuries has been dubbed the "nadir," the "capitulation to racism," and the "dark journey."[5] It is a painful and often ugly and sordid story, deeply compromising cherished American principles of democracy, equal justice, and equal opportunity. It is the story of a people denied the basic rights of citizenship in the land of their birth, yet fully expected to stay in their "place" and to display as much patriotism, loyalty, and valor on the battlefield in defense of those rights as their white countrymen, who enjoyed the full exercise of such rights. It is the story of a people stamped as racially inferior, yet fully expected to provide the most demanding labor of the South even as they complied with the perverse etiquette of Jim Crow. It is the story of how white Southerners defended, tolerated, and rationalized the systematic abuse and exploitation of black men and women in the name of ensuring their own supremacy, security, and profits. To suggest that their story is simply another version of the classic struggle of all immigrants ignores the distinctiveness of the African American experience, the unique and overwhelming obstacles blacks faced, and the indignities, humiliations, and violence they were forced to endure. America was founded on the principle and reality of white supremacy and the notion of black inferiority and black unfreedom—a notion that each new wave of immigrants assimilated as quickly as the epithet "nigger."

Rather than face up to their history, however, Americans found refuge and comfort in a highly selective memory that refused to acknowledge the experience of black people as part of the American heritage. For centuries, enslaved labor, segregation, lynching, terrorism, discrimination, and every form of humiliation and brutalization imaginable took a heavy toll on black lives, particularly in the South. But Americans chose to think themselves immune not only to history but to the lessons of history. "In the underground of our unwritten history," wrote black novelist Ralph Ellison, "much of that which is ignored defies our inattention by continuing to grow and have consequences."[6]

The black odyssey includes some of the bleakest examples of repression in the history of this nation. But it is at the same time a story of extraordinary resilience, the story (as Nathan Huggins wrote) of "a people who had to endure and make choices under conditions and circumstances which are outside our experience to know . . . , whose courage was in their refusal to be brutes, in their insistence on holding themselves together, on acting, speaking, and singing as men and women."[7] It is a story of resistance, defined not so much by spectacular feats and insurrections as by day-to-day acts, employing various forms of expression, often subtle and individual. In Ralph Ellison's *Invisible Man*, the protagonist's grandfather makes a deathbed confession. "Son, after I'm gone I want you to keep up the good fight. I never told you, but our life is a war and I have been a traitor all my born days, a spy in the enemy's country ever since I give up my gun back in the Reconstruction." He then admonishes his grandson, "Live with your head in the lion's mouth. I want you to overcome 'em with yeses, undermine 'em with grins, agree 'em to death and destruction, let 'em swoller you till they vomit or bust wide open."[8] How many black Southerners adopted the grandfather's advice will never be known with any certainty, but scores of black men and women acted in that spirit, determined "to overcome 'em with yeses" and "undermine 'em with grins."

Half-a-century after the Emancipation Proclamation, some 90 percent of black Americans still lived in the South, and the dominant racial attitudes were nothing less than religious and moral commandments. Reconstruction had been over for more than a decade, much longer in most states, but the experience of biracial, democratic government reminded whites of the urgent need to keep blacks in their place. That memory of the past—black men learning the uses of political power—went far to shape the racial boundaries and ideology of the New South and encouraged the use of terrorist violence to rout any further challenge to white supremacy.

If most Southern whites quickly adapted to the post-Reconstruction economic and political order, that was because much of the old order had been reestablished. The traumatic experiences of emancipation and Reconstruction were not soon forgotten, but whites reaffirmed their confidence that they alone knew and understood their "nigras" and how to deal with them; indeed, that conviction became more insistent even as it became less credible. It was the last line of defense against "outsiders" who sought to unsettle and agitate an ostensibly cheerful and acquiescent black population.

But that intimate knowledge claimed by whites rested by and large on the assumption that black lives were transparent, devoid of any real depth or complexity. It seemed to David L. Cohn, a native white who spent his boyhood in the Mississippi Delta, that "nearly all white Southerners" shared "a general delusion" about Negroes: that because they lived among them, employed them as cooks, maids, nurses, and washerwomen, they intimately understood Negro life and character. But Cohn himself readily conceded that he possessed no such knowledge, and he believed few of his white neighbors did, no matter what they said to the contrary. "The truth is, most Southern whites have only the faintest comprehension of the inner lives of Negroes which remain forever secret and alien to them."[9]

No matter how many times whites reassured themselves about their unique gift of comprehending Negroes, many came to concede, as did Cohn, that they knew only what blacks chose to reveal—and that was remarkably little. It was a lesson some whites had learned during the Civil War, and it had stunned them. The very blacks they thought they knew best were often the ones they knew least of all; they had mistaken the outward demeanor of "their" black folk for the blacks' inner feelings; they had read docility as contentment, deference and accommodation as submission. "The Southerners say we negroes are a happy, laughing set of people, with no thought of tomorrow," a woman reflected, "How mistaken they are." To endure, often to survive, many blacks had learned from experience to anticipate the white family's moods and whims, to know its expectations, to placate and exploit its fears and apprehensions, and at the same time to mask their own emotions and views. When questioned about politics or about the war, many a black carefully framed his response. "Why, you see master," an elderly Louisiana slave told a Union reporter in 1863, "'taint for an old nigger like me to know anything 'bout politics." The reporter persisted, however, demanding to know if the slave supported the Confederacy or the Union. With an "ineffable smile" and mock gravity, the slave announced, "I'm on de Lord's side, and He'll work out His salvation, bress de Lord."[10]

No doubt some blacks internalized the arts of evasion and accommodation, acknowledging the pervasiveness of white power. "You just automatically grow up inferior," Charles Gratton, a black Alabaman, recalled, "and you had the feeling that white people were better than you. It just really wasn't any question asked then about why."[11] Some years later, in a folktale that passed through various versions, a four-year-old black boy was asked what he wanted to be when he grew up. "A white man," he responded without hesitation — "'Cause my momma says a nigger ain't worth shit."[12] On the other hand, many blacks recalled being raised by parents who insisted they were in no way inferior to whites, and some, like Richard Wright, born in 1908 in a sharecropper's cabin near Natchez, Mississippi, maintained their self-esteem even as children. Wright firmly rejected the notion that white folks somehow understood blacks better than blacks understood themselves.

> The white South said that it knew "niggers," and I was what the white South called a "nigger." Well, the white South had never known me—never known what I thought, what I felt. The white South said that I had a "place" in life. Well, I had never felt my "place"; or, rather, my deepest instincts had always made me reject the "place" to which the white South had assigned me. It had never occurred to me that I was in any way an inferior being, and no word that I had ever heard fall from the lips of southern white men had ever made me really doubt the worth of my own humanity. True, I had lied. I had stolen. I had struggled to contain my seething anger. I had fought, and it was perhaps a mere accident that I had never killed. . . . But in what other ways had the South allowed me to be natural, to be real, to be myself, except in rejection, rebellion, and aggression?[13]

For most blacks, how they acted in the presence of whites depended on their perception of reality and where power rested in the small world to which they were confined. Not only were they to be respectful and suppress any anger they felt, but they learned never to question the veracity of whites or behave in any manner that might be construed as "sassiness" or "impudence." If cursed, they were never to return the insult. If struck, they were to avoid any retaliation. Whatever the provocation, they needed to guard their reactions carefully.

Richard Wright's boyhood friend admonished him, "For God's sake, learn how to live in the South! . . . You act around white people as if you didn't know that they were white. And they *see* it. . . . When you're in front of white people, *think* before you act, *think* before you speak." To be a "good Negro" was to act with the utmost restraint and deference, to veil one's inner feelings. What Ralph Ellison wrote of the "mask of meekness" assumed by slaves was no less true of the one assumed by blacks maneuvering to survive in the worst days of Jim Crow. The "mask of meekness," Ellison suggested, "conceals the wisdom of one who has learned the secret of saying the 'yes' which accomplishes the expressive 'no.'"[14] Generations of blacks made the same point when they taught their children, "Be sho' you knows 'bout all you tells but don't tell all you knows," or when the bluesman sang

Well, I drink to keep from worryin' and I laugh to
    keep from cryin'
Well, I drink to keep from worryin' and I laugh to
    keep from cryin'
I keep a smile on my face so the public won't know
    my mind.

Some people thinks I'm happy but they sho' don't
    know my mind,
Some people thinks I'm happy but they sho' don't
    know my mind,
They see this smile on my face, but my heart is
    bleeding all the time.[15]

All too many blacks had shared the experience of Willie Harrell, born in 1927, a sharecropper in Mississippi, and like the generations before him dependent on his employers for food and supplies. That dependency circumscribed his day-to-day life and ruled out any prospect of improving his position. He learned to grow crops. "That's all we knowed about. All we ever did [was] farmed." Having few options, he also learned to obey the racial rules. He knew that the only way to enter a white family's home was through the back door. He knew to respond when addressed as "son" or "boy" or "Harrell." "That's all they ever knowed of my name," and they called the older people "Uncle" or "Auntie." He remained illiterate, since he would have had to walk seven or eight miles to the nearest school and could attend classes only when bad weather made fieldwork impossible — "two days out of a month or a year." He quickly learned how to behave in the presence of whites, most urgently in the presence of white women. "Shit, you couldn't even look at a white woman hard back then when I come up. You would get hung. Yeah. Sure would. . . . But whites could look at blacks all they wanted." To attempt to leave the place where he labored was to invite a brutal beating. "Wasn't nothing you could do, but take it. You try to resist [and] they would kill you. [It was] just like I'm in prison or something. [They were] watching you. [You] couldn't go nowhere." But one night Willie Harrell managed to escape, making his way past the electrified fence. "I couldn't take no more of it. [I] got tired of it. I got to git, and I got, too. . . . [If] I'd have stayed on down there, they would have killed me."[16]

Seeing only a demeanor of contentment, the grin and

the shuffle, some whites might have been thinking all was well with the black folks they claimed to know so intimately. But many demanded reassurances. Despite their public professions of confidence in the "good Negroes," white Southerners failed to find the racial security they so desperately sought. Not only did they remain obsessed with the need to police the Negro community; they focused their attention on the behavior, movement, and demeanor of certain Negroes in particular—the children and grandchildren of former slaves, those who with alarming regularity refused to stay in their place, who appeared to be less in awe of whites, and who were less inclined to respect the old racial mores. In 1913, a Mississippi senator sadly observed how the "grand old darky" was being replaced by "the Afro-American, which means a good servant girl or a good farm hand spoiled."[17]

During the years 1890 to 1915, in response to perceptions of a "New Negro," born in freedom, undisciplined by slavery and unschooled in racial etiquette, and in response to growing doubts that this new generation could be trusted to stay in its place without legal force, the white South denied blacks a political voice through disfranchisement, imposed rigid patterns of racial segregation (Jim Crow), sustained an economic system—sharecropping and tenantry—that left little room for ambition or hope, refused blacks equal educational resources (W. E. B. Du Bois called it "enforced ignorance"), manipulated and perverted the judicial system, sustained extraordinary and unprecedented levels of violence and brutality, and disseminated racial caricatures and pseudo-scientific theories that reinforced and comforted whites in their racial beliefs and practices. This was the work not of racial demagogues but of the "best people"—the most educated, the most refined, the most respected.

When the white South acted on its racial creed, it sought to impress upon black people their political and economic powerlessness and vulnerability, to diminish their self-esteem and their aspirations. Jim Crow was everywhere, instructing blacks as to where they could legally reside, walk, sit, rest, eat, drink, work, seek entertainment, be hospitalized, and be buried. In some public parks, signs refused admission to "Negroes and Dogs"; in Texas, the exclusion extended as well to Mexicans. For most whites, it was simply a matter of reigning in troublesome and obnoxious inferiors. "The white people began to begrudge these niggers their running around and doing just as they chose," recalled Sam Gadsden, a black South Carolinian born in 1882. "That's all there is to segregation, that caused the whole thing. The white people couldn't master these niggers any more, so they took up the task of intimidating them."[18]

Not only were they to be intimidated into submission but they were to be policed, so there would be no doubt they fully understood their place in Southern society. Jim Crow was not limited to statutory restrictions but had come to be embedded in custom and tradition. If blacks ventured into unfamiliar territory, for example, they needed to be doubly cautious about their movements and always sensitive to local ways. The "unwritten law" in the rural South, as in much of the North and West, dictated that a white resident had to be able to vouch for the character of Negroes unknown to the community. This meant that a black stranger could be stopped anywhere at any time and forced to state his business to the satisfaction of any white questioner. If the stranger provided the wrong answer or replied in a manner less than deferential, he was likely to be arrested or forcibly removed. After sunset, entire communities and the areas surrounding them might be off limits to blacks. Although this "law" was enforced especially rigidly in the South, it was directed at blacks throughout the United States. No matter where black people traveled, they had to assess the racial terrain and determine where their presence could invite trouble. "Nigger, don't let the sun go down on you here" might be a posted warning ("Nigger—Read and Run") or a verbal curse; in either case, whites enforced the prohibition. "Sundown towns," as they came to be called, dotted the American landscape well into the twenty-first century, underscoring how custom trumped law and how racial proscription transcended geography. If the term enjoyed less popularity in the East, white residents still found ways to maintain its spirit. Some communities qualified as "sundown towns" only after forcibly driving the black residents (and often other ethnic and racial groups) into exile.[19]

The refusal of whites to commingle on equal terms with black men and women rested on whites' fears of any form of racial coexistence that threatened the unquestioning domination of the white race. Alfred H. Stone, a leading white Mississippian and former slaveholder, claimed that Southern whites had no objection to personal association with Negroes, "provided it be upon terms which contain no suggestion of equality of personal status."[20] That was the imperative. That was why the proscription of blacks had to be imposed upon black voters. Disfranchisement came to the South in the 1890s and early twentieth century because black political participation revived memories of Radical Reconstruction and remained linked in the white mind with black ambition, social equality, and miscegenation. To bar the black man from the polling place was to bar him from the bedroom. In erecting the new barriers to black voting, whites circumvented the Fifteenth Amendment by establishing literacy and property requirements. But, in practice, it made no difference which class of blacks exercised the vote; the more literate and intelligent the black voter, the greater the danger he posed and the more apt he was to transform political into social equality. "I am just as much opposed to Booker Washington as a voter, with all his Anglo-Saxon reinforcements," James K. Vardaman of Mississippi insisted, "as I am to the cocoanut-headed, chocolate-covered, typical little coon, Andy Dotson, who blacks my shoes every morning. Neither is fit to perform the supreme function of citizenship."[21] Such opinions quickly disposed of the argument advanced by black accommodationists that blacks would educate themselves back into the polling place. No matter what strides blacks made in education, whites—by law and violence—resisted black political participation. After all, as one newspaper expressed the prevailing white sentiment, "They do not object to negroes voting on account of ignorance, but on account of color."[22]

The mechanics of repression, the ritualized and institutionalized subordination demanded of blacks, exacted a psychological and physical toll, shaping day-to-day black life and demeanor to an extraordinary degree. Perhaps the most difficult revelation for a new generation of blacks to absorb was that color marked them as inferior in the eyes of whites, no matter how they behaved, how much deference they displayed, or what social class they belonged to.

> Our seedy run-down school told us that if we had any place at all in the scheme of things it was a separate place, marked off, proscribed and unwanted by the white people. We were bottled up and labeled and set aside — sent to the Jim Crow car, the back of the bus, the side door of the theater, the side window of a restaurant. We came to know that whatever we had was always inferior. We came to understand that no matter how neat and clean, how law abiding, submissive and polite, how studious in school, how churchgoing and moral, how scrupulous in paying our bills and taxes we were, it made no essential difference in our place.[23]

What happened in the courts of law underscored and reinforced the actions of legislators and public officials. The entire machinery of justice — the lawyers, the judges, the juries, the legal profession, the police — functioned as a formidable instrument of social control, operating with ruthless efficiency to uphold the absolute power of whites to command the subordination and labor of blacks. The criminal and civil codes implied that the legal system was color blind. "Nothing could be further from the truth," insisted Sidney Davis, a circuit court judge in Mississippi in the 1920s.[24] Unwritten, based on experience and custom, "Negro" law applied to much of the South. Police officers, judges, lawyers, and jurors understood that in the daily enforcement of the law, some statutes applied to both races, some only to whites, some only to blacks. The courts excluded blacks from juries, disregarded black testimony, and meted out sentences based less on the evidence than on the race of the defendant—or, as a New Orleans black newspaper said of one unfortunate black defendant, after he had been given a ninety-day sentence, he was sentenced "3 days for stealing and 87 days for being colored."[25] All too often, however, the black defendant had difficulty discerning the offenses he had allegedly committed.

> Got me accused of peepin'—I can't even see a thing,
> Got me accused of beggin'—I can't even raise my
>   hand.
>
> Bad luck, bad luck is killin' me,
> I just can't stand no more of this third degree.
>
> Got me accused of taxes, I don't have a lousy dime,
> Got me accused of children an' nary one of them is
>   mine.

Got me accused of murder, I never harmed a man,
Got me accused of forgery, I can't even write my
    name.[26]

The story that resonated with truth among blacks told
of a judge who tried to stop a lynch mob by pleading
with them, "We've always been considered a progressive
community and I think we're progressive enough so's
we can give this boy a fair trial and then lynch him."[27]
Nearly every black person suspected such judges were
common. With equal cynicism, blacks understood that
though the courts dealt severely with blacks accused of
crimes against white persons or property, they often
chose to ignore black violence against blacks. "If a nigger
kills a white man, that's murder," a chief of police explained. "If a white man kills a nigger, that's justifiable
homicide. If a nigger kills another nigger, that's one less
nigger."[28]

The most repressive period in the history of race relations was also the most violent. Efforts to enforce black
deference and solidify the subordination of black men
and women knew no apparent limits. As late as 1937, social psychologist John Dollard could write, "Every Negro
in the South knows that he is under a kind of sentence of
death; he does not know when his turn will come, it may
never come, but it may also be any time."[29] Sometimes
in small groups, sometimes in massive numbers, white
mobs combined the roles of judge, jury, and executioner.
Only in recent years have white Americans come to rec-

ognize the full dimensions of the violence that gripped the South in the late nineteenth and early twentieth centuries, when some two or three black Southerners were hanged, burned at the stake, or quietly murdered every week. Between 1882 and 1968, what Richard Wright would call the "white death" took the lives of an estimated 4,742 blacks.[30] Just as many, if not more, were victims of legal lynchings (speedy trials and executions), private white violence, and "nigger hunts," murdered by various means in isolated rural areas and dumped into rivers and creeks. Ann Pointer, the youngest of six children of tenant farmers in Macon County, Alabama, recalled the number of times "white people [would] get mad with someone on their farm and kill them and throw them in the creek." In one incident, a black body washed up near her family's farm. "They said the sheriff killed him. I ain't never found out why, but it was so many things happening around here. It isn't a lynching, just a killing."[31]

Many of the victims of lynchings had not assimilated the rituals of deference and submission; some had challenged or unintentionally violated the prevailing norms of white supremacy; and still others, innocent of any crime or offense, were lynched because they were black and in the wrong place at the wrong time. Bluesman "Big Bill" Broonzy recalled the fate of an uncle who had the audacity to voice his complaints. "They hung him down there because they say he was crazy and he might ruin the other Negroes. See? And that is why they hung him, see, because he was the man that if he worked, he wanted pay."[32] Men and women, young and old, were lynched. Laura Nelson and her teenage son were wrongly accused of murdering a deputy sheriff. Removed from the local jail by a mob in Okemah, Oklahoma, in 1911, they were hung together from a bridge, the mother swaying some twenty feet away from her son.[33]

Every lynching was intended to drive home a warning to the black community about the consequences of resistance, no matter how muted it might be. This was sometimes achieved by dragging the victim through the black section of town; leaving the dismembered body to dangle for several days in public view, tied to a tree, a lamppost, or a bridge; or placing the body on a railroad track so that passing trains could make their mark on the corpse.

Nothing so dramatically underscored the perceived cheapness of black lives in the white South. The abolition of slaves as private property expedited the transition from white brutality to white savagery. The sadism and exhibitionism transformed lynchings into public theater, voyeuristic rituals of torture and death. Perhaps "rednecks," "crackers," and "peckerwoods" played a more public role, but the lynchers and the spectators who applauded their actions came together in an impressive display of racial and community solidarity. Drawn from all classes, most of them were ordinary, respectable, churchgoing folk. In the vast majority of lynchings, the coroners' juries concluded routinely (often as rapidly as the lynchings had occurred) that the victims had met their deaths "at the hands of unknown parties." Few members of a lynch mob were ever apprehended, and only rarely did the leaders or the participants seek to conceal their identity. The conspiracy of silence made entire communities complicit in murder.

On a Sunday afternoon in 1899, excursion trains carried spectators to Newman, Georgia, to see Sam Hose burned alive. Like so many lynchings, this was nothing less than ritualized murder. After his ears, toes, and fingers were cut off, they were distributed among the crowd as souvenirs; his eyes were then gouged from their sockets, his tongue torn out, his heart removed and sliced up, his flesh cut with knives. The crowd fought over the body parts. His severed knuckles would be prominently displayed in the window of an Atlanta grocery store.[34]

The same sense of publicly sanctioned justice informed the crowd that assembled in 1918 in Valdosta, Georgia, to lynch Mary Turner—in her eighth month of pregnancy. She had vowed to swear out warrants against the mob leaders who murdered her husband. As punishment for making the threat, a mob of several hundred hung her from a tree, head downward. While she was still alive, someone used a knife ordinarily reserved for splitting hogs to cut open the woman's abdomen. The infant fell prematurely from her womb to the ground and cried briefly, whereupon a member of the mob crushed the baby's head beneath his heel. Mary Turner was then shot and hanged.[35]

Lynching rituals were acted out in every part of the South. Newspapers spared none of the pornographic details. Photographers were there to record the event for

posterity and profit; they captured the carnival-like atmo-
sphere, as in the lynching of Thomas Brooks in Fayette
County, Tennessee, in 1915:

> Hundreds of kodaks clicked all morning at the scene
> of the lynching. People in automobiles and carriages
> came from miles around to view the corpse dangling
> from the end of a rope under the Nashville, Chatta-
> nooga & St. Louis Railway bridge. Picture card pho-
> tographers installed a portable printing plant at the
> bridge and reaped a harvest in selling postcards show-
> ing a photograph of the lynched Negro.
>
> Women and children were there by the score. At a
> number of country schools the day's routine was de-
> layed until boy and girl pupils could get back from
> viewing the lynched man.

Hanged from the trestlework supporting the bridge,
Brooks's body was left to dangle over the public high-
way, "suspended low enough for travelers along the road
to-day to reach up and spin the corpse around."[36] After
a lynching in Robinson, Texas, in 1916, an observer
penned on the back of the postcard photo, "This is the
Barbecue we had last night my picture is to the left with
a cross over it." He signed it, "your son Joe." The photo
depicted the charred body of Jesse Washington, burned
alive before a crowd of fifteen thousand.[37]

The people who tortured and murdered in this fashion understood what they were doing. This was not the
outburst of crazed men but the triumph of a belief system that defined a people not only as inferior but as less

than human. For the men and women who constituted these mobs, as for those who remained silent and indifferent or who provided the scholarly and scientific explanations, this was the highest idealism in the service of their race. One has only to view the self-satisfied expressions on their faces as they posed for photographs beneath black bodies hanging from a tree or beside the charred remains of a Negro. This is not an easy history to absorb. The images and details can numb the mind, deaden the senses; they tax our sense of who we are and who we have been. No wonder lynchings occupy such a small place in our historical literature and textbooks. The omission has been called a "double lynching" because it also murdered any memory of the crime.

The experience of black Southerners mocked a fundamental assumption of the American Dream: that through their industry, skill, and enterprise they would gain recognition and share political and economic power. From their first days of freedom, they were forcibly reminded that lofty ambitions and evidence of advancement might be resented and resisted. While maintaining that blacks were incapable of becoming their social, political, or economic equals, the dominant society betrayed the fear that they might. Even as whites scorned black incompetence, they feared evidence of black competence, assertion, independence, and ambition. When Richard Wright sought training in optometry, he was admonished by the white men who would have to teach him: "What are you trying to do, get smart, nigger?"[38]

No wonder many blacks came to believe that it was futile to work hard and obtain wealth and property. The "man" would somehow find a way to deprive them of their gains, whether by fraud, intimidation, or violence, as this bluesman suggested:

Ain't it hard, ain't it hard,
Ain't it hard, to be a nigger, nigger, nigger?
Ain't it hard, ain't it hard?
For you can't git yo' money when it's due.

Well, it make no difference,
    How you make out yo' time;
White man sho bring a
    Nigger out behin'.

Nigger an' white man
    Playin' seven-up;
Nigger win de money—
    Skeered to pick 'em up.

If you work all the week,
    An' work all the time,
White man sho to bring
    Nigger out behin'.[39]

The Class of 1886 at Tuskegee Institute felt sufficiently confident about their prospects to adopt as their motto, "There Is Room at the Top." But in the town of Tuskegee, the danger of success was readily acknowledged by a black resident: "I know men who won't keep a horse. If they get one they will sell it. If you ask him why he sold his horse he very likely will say: 'A white man see me in dat 'ere horse, he look hard at me. I make [up] my min' a mule good 'nough for a ole nigger like me."[40]

Tom Moss of Memphis had saved his money as a letter carrier, and with two other black men opened a store in the suburbs. In 1892 he and his partners were murdered by a mob because "they were succeeding too well. They were guilty of no crime but that." After the murder of the three men, a mob looted the store, creditors closed the place, and what remained of the stock was sold at auction.[41]

Richard Wright was eight years old when white men murdered his Uncle Hoskins in the saloon he owned in Elaine, Arkansas. Local whites had long resented and coveted his uncle's flourishing business. Ignoring warnings and death threats, he determined to stay longer and make more money. "There was no funeral," Wright recalled. "There was no music. There was no period of mourning. There were no flowers. There were only silence, quiet weeping, whispers, and fear. . . . This was as close as white terror had ever come to me and my mind reeled. Why had we not fought back, I asked my mother, and the fear that was in her made her slap me into silence.[42]

Eunice Rivers witnessed her father intimidated into submission. "He was just living a little bit too well to be a Negro, see. A Negro's s'posed to be in a little cabin, and the white man tell him when to go and when to come. Well, Papa couldn't stand that."[43]

Audley Moore was aware that her grandfather had been lynched for "standing up to some white people" who coveted his land. "This was all it amounted to, because after he was lynched they ran my grandmother off the land, and she had to take her five little children and flee for her life with the things they had on their back, nothing else, leave everything."[44]

Fear of black success persisted well into the twentieth century. Civil rights leader Fanny Lou Hamer, born in Mississippi in 1917, recalled how her father kept working as a sharecropper until he had saved enough to purchase some wagons, plowing tools, and mules. But whites came to her father's lot and poisoned the mules. "It killed everything we had. . . . That poisoning knocked us right back down flat. We never did get back up again. That white man did it just because we were getting somewhere. White people never like to see Negroes get a little success."[45]

White farmers (known as "whitecappers") terrorized black farmers off land they rented or had managed to purchase. "They wanted to run me off on account of my crop," a Mississippi farmer testified. "They took everything I had, and all my wife had, and broke us teetotally up." Incidents of white violence had a way of increasing in the summer months, after blacks had planted their crops. "Now is the season," explained a Georgia editor, "when the tenant with the best crop gets run off the place."[46]

Few understood better than Ned Cobb, an Alabama farmer born in 1885, how whites resented black success. Through persistence and hard work, Cobb managed to accumulate property. But to keep the property was a continual struggle, demanding more resourcefulness and energy than he had expended to acquire it. "I had men to turn me down, wouldn't let me have the land I needed to work, wouldn't sell me guano, didn't want to see me with anything. Soon as I got to where I could have somethin for sure and was makin somethin of myself, then they commenced a runnin at me." Public signs of success (for example, Ned Cobb driving about town in a buggy) mostly infuriated local whites. The reason, Cobb explained, was that white people "hated to see niggers livin like people." Blacks who accumulated property or money would become independent, and whites feared the consequences. "Afraid a nigger might do somethin if he got the money in his own hands, do as he please; might hold on to it if he wanted to hold it, might spend it according to his pleasure. The white people was afraid I'll say this: they was afraid the money would make the nigger act too much like his own man." Perhaps, then, the way to survive in the South was to avoid accumulating enough to arouse white resentment. The unsuccessful black man posed no threat; he knew his place. Cobb described his own father as such a man. "He had money but—whenever the colored man prospered too fast in his country under the old rulins, they worked every figure to cut you down, cut your britches off you. So, it might have been to his way of thinkin that it weren't no use in climbin too fast; weren't no use in climbin slow, neither, if they was goin to take everything you worked for when you got too high." Ned Cobb's brother adopted that lesson as a way of life. "He made up his mind that he weren't goin to have anything and after that, why, nothin could hurt him."[47]

Even as black leaders such as Booker T. Washington

clung to their faith in self-help, W. E. B. Du Bois came to appreciate the tragic flaw in the Gospel of Success. Moving up in the world was reserved for whites only—at least, some whites. The historical evidence fully supported the grim conclusion Du Bois reached in the aftermath of the 1906 Atlanta "riot," namely that the violence was directed less at the vagabond or the criminal black than at the successful and ambitious black—"the negro who is coming forward."

> If my own city of Atlanta [was] offered . . . to-day the choice between 500 Negro college graduates—forceful, busy, ambitious men of property and self-respect—and 500 black cringing vagrants and criminals, the popular vote in favor of the criminals would be simply overwhelming. Why? because they want Negro crime? No, not that they fear Negro crime less, but that they fear Negro ambition and success more. They can deal with crime by chain-gang and lynch law, or at least they think they can, but the South can conceive neither machinery nor place for the educated, self-reliant, self-assertive black man.[48]

In Atlanta in 1906, white mobs spent four days murdering and assaulting blacks and plundering black homes and shops—and much of the violence fell on the most successful, educated, and accommodating blacks. The middle-class neighborhood in which they lived became a natural target of the mobs, the place to teach overly ambitious blacks lessons they would never forget.

Among those driven from their homes was Dr. W. F. Penn, a prominent black physician, a graduate of Yale, a man who commanded influence in the community. In the aftermath of the riot, he asked a group of prominent Atlanta whites, "How shall we protect our lives and property?"

> If living a sober, industrious, upright life, accumulating property and educating his children as best he knows how, is not the standard by which a colored man can live and be protected in the South, what is to become of him? When we aspire to be decent and industrious we are told that we are bad examples to other colored men. Tell us what your standards are for colored men. What are the requirements under which we may live and be protected? What shall we do?[49]

At the turn of the twentieth century, in the face of growing white hostility, violence, and both legal and extralegal repression, blacks drew inward, constructing in their communities a separate world with its own businesses, fraternal organizations, churches, schools, newspapers, and community institutions—in many ways, a replica of the society that excluded them. Within rigidly prescribed boundaries, they improvised strategies and tried to deal pragmatically with life as they found it. With the normal outlets of expression and protest closed to them, black men and women were forced to find alternative ways (verbal and nonverbal) to articulate their concerns and feelings. None did so more eloquently than the bluesmen and blueswomen, singing songs that Langston Hughes described as "sadder even than the spirituals, because their sadness is not softened with tears but hardened with laughter, the absurd, incongruous laughter of a sadness without even a god to appeal to."[50]

The men and women who played and sang the blues were mostly poor, propertyless, disreputable ramblers, many of them illiterate, loners, living on the edge. They could be heard on street corners, at dances, in train stations, cafés, juke joints, and brothels. When Big Bill Broonzy and Memphis Slim sang the blues, as they recalled, they were aware that others in the audience whom they did not know personally nonetheless shared their feelings. Among other things, the blues afforded them the rare opportunity to communicate in song impressions (sometimes coded) of white folks that were otherwise dangerous to impart.

> *Big Bill:* I've known guys that wanted to cuss out the boss and he was afraid to go up to his face and tell him what he wanted to tell him, and I've heard him sing those things—sing words, you know—back to the boss.
> *Memphis:* Yeah, blues is kind of revenge, you know. You wanta say something, and you wanta, you know, signifyin' like—that's the blues, like a, you know, we all fellers, we had a hard time in life and like that, and things we couldn't say or do, so we sing it. I mean we sing.[51]

What bound the performers to their audiences were shared experiences and a common history and culture; they gave voice to the anxieties, the dissatisfactions of marginalized people, some of whom had resigned themselves to living without hope, to enjoying the moment without looking past it. The blues, on the other hand, could be liberating, enabling people to withstand, even transcend the pain of living.

The blues captured eloquently and compellingly the entrapment of many black men and women in the age of Jim Crow, the formidable obstacles they faced in a constant struggle to survive. In "High Water Everywhere," Charlie Patton, bluesman, preacher, and field laborer on Will Dockery's plantation in the Mississippi Delta, describes the devastating flood of 1927. The levees gave way at several places on the Mississippi River, forcing the evacuation of scores of black families and their confinement in hastily built tent cities. The plight of the refugees only underscored their vulnerability; they were left to be washed away by circumstances over which they had no control, at the mercy of a pernicious system of racial coercion and injustice that in this instance impeded rescue and relief efforts.

> Backwater at Blytheville, doctor weren't around
> Backwater at Blytheville, done took Joiner town
> It was fifty families (*Spoken:* and children) suffer to
>   sink and drown.
>
> The water was risin' up at my friend's door
> The water was risin' up at my friend's door
> The man said to his womenfolk, Lord, we'd better go.
>
> The water was risin', got up in my bed
> Lord, the water it rollin', got up to my bed

I thought I would take a trip, Lord, out on a big ice
    sled.

Oh I hear, Lord Lord, water upon my door
    (*Spoken:* You know what I mean?)
I hear the ice boat, Lord, went sinkin' down
I couldn't get no closer, Marion City gone down.

So high the water was risin', I been sinkin' down
Then the water was risin', at places all around
    (*Spoken:* Boy, they's all around)
It was fifty men and children, come to sink and
    drown.

Oh, Lord, oh lordy, women and grown men down
Ohhh, women an' children sinkin' down
    (*Spoken:* Lord have mercy)
I couldn't see nobody home and wasn't no one to be
    found.[52]

To a remarkable degree, the blues enabled a new generation of severely repressed, Jim Crowed black Southerners to express, in the words of Ralph Ellison, "both the agony of life and the possibility of conquering it through sheer toughness of spirit," as in the despair voiced by this Memphis bluesman:

What you going to do, Mama,
When your troubles get like mine.
Take a mouthful of sugar,
and drink a bottle of turpentine.
I can't stand it,
I can't stand it.

Drop down, Mama,
Sweet as the showers of rain.[53]

And few could match the emotional depths plumbed by
Bertha "Chippie" Hill in her plaintive, poignant, chilling lament: "I'm gonna lay my head on a lonesome railroad line/and let the 2:19 pacify my mind."[54]

Like the blues, humor—"the kind of humor that
laughs to keep from crying"—voiced the tensions of people caught in a marginal world and helped them to deal
with limited options in their daily lives. Both blues and
humor shared a common theme: the betrayal of expectations, the belief that the success creed was for white folks
only. Even when blacks played by the rules and did everything demanded of them (as black leaders and white
philanthropists advised), the results were much the same.
In fact, when blacks entered the contest, the rules often
changed, and the mythical level playing field developed
deep cracks—as this story, passed on in various versions
from generation to generation, suggests:

After the Lord had created the Earth, he created the
white man, the Mexican, and the Negro. So one day
he told them, "Go out and get you some rocks." The
white man, being industrious, went out and got a huge
rock. The Mexican got a middle-sized rock, and the
Negro, being lazy, got a pebble. Later on that evening, the Lord said, "I'm going to turn these rocks into
bread." As a result, the white man had a lot of bread,
the Mexican had a sufficient amount, but the Negro
only had a crumb, and he stayed hungry. So the next

day, the Lord again told them the same thing. This time the white man got a great big rock, the Mexican a little smaller rock, but the Negro brought back a whole half of a mountain. That evening the Lord stood before them and said, "Upon this rock, I will build my church." The Negro said, "You're a mother-fucking liar, you're going to make me some bread."[55]

Few speeches or editorials made the point with greater eloquence. The story suggests a perception of white America as unbeatable, an arena where the rules and laws are made, enforced, and broken by the same men. This is a familiar theme in the black experience. To succeed is to fail. There is no way to win.

Terrorism reinforced a racism whites expressed in various ways on a day-to-day basis. It was impressed upon blacks through lynchings or through economic coercion—the ways in which whites made certain that blacks would find it difficult to succeed. The story that follows surfaced in the 1930s, but the realities it depicts mirror the experiences of blacks, probably a sizable majority, for much of the twentieth century.

A white man and a black man happened upon two boxes at a rural crossroads (where so much seems to occur in Southern black lore). Having spotted the boxes first, the black man ran ahead and opted for the larger box. Upon opening it, he found picks, shovels, and hoes. He then turned around to see how the white man had fared. "Well de Wite man he got de little box and when he open hit dar war pens an pencils an paper an er big count book wat he keeps wat de niggers owes em in. And dats de way hits been eber since. De Nigger just caint outfigger de Wite man for he sure ter cut yer down."[56]

The pens and pencils put the finishing touches on a system of coercive labor in which blacks enjoyed neither ownership of the land nor the full rewards of their toil. The cycle of work, debt, and poverty became as routinized as the labor performed. Time after time, the black laborer came away owing more than he had made, forcing him to deal with the same merchant and landlord for still another year. There appeared to be no way out. "I have been living in this Delta thirty years," a Mississippi sharecropper revealed, "and I know that I have been robbed every year; but there is no use jumping out of the frying pan into the fire. If we ask any questions we are cussed, and if we raise up we are shot, and that ends it."[57]

Racism helped to explain and undergird economic exploitation, but it was grounded in ideas and stereotypes highly popular throughout the country and shared by whites of all classes and national origins. If mobs lynched blacks with calculated sadistic cruelty, historians and the academic sciences were no less resourceful in providing the intellectual underpinnings of racist thought and behavior, validating theories of black degeneracy and cultural and intellectual inferiority. Newspaper caricatures, popular literature, minstrel shows, and vaudeville depicted blacks as a race of buffoons and half-wits, and with D. W. Griffith's *Birth of a Nation* in 1915, the cinema did more than any historian to explain the "Negro problem" to the American people—the dangers (vividly depicted on the screen) posed by a race freed from the restraints of slavery. Beneath the grinning acquiescence of the black man, the film warned, there lurks a mindless savagery that demands white vigilance—and, if necessary, vigilantes. Milton Quigless, a sleeping-car porter and physician raised in Port Gibson, Mississippi, recalled watching the movie from the "nigger gallery." He heard the crowd below him cheer when whites took their vengeance on blacks and reestablished white supremacy. "I'll never forget it. I really saw what it was all about . . . and, man, they got mean as hell. The White folks got meaner.[58]

In 1913, the year Woodrow Wilson was inaugurated president of the United States, black Americans celebrated the fiftieth anniversary of the Emancipation Proclamation. Over the previous half century, black Southerners, acting on their newly won freedom, had made significant progress in farm and home ownership, in business enterprise, in the professions, in the accumulation of wealth, and in the dramatic reduction of illiteracy (from 90 percent in 1865 to 30 percent in 1913). Black leaders and editors cited such progress to justify emancipation and to validate black potential. White Southerners were less certain. Some questioned the evidence; some feared it; most remained insistent on the need to subordinate blacks—the unsuccessful and the successful—to a white-dominated and white-managed social and economic order. But black leaders vowed from the outset of World

War I that the old racial hierarchy would not survive this conflict. One Mississippi-born graduate of Tuskegee Institute told an overflow crowd in a Memphis church: "You may burn me, but you cannot burn away my record of undying loyalty. You may shake the rope in my face, but no rope is strong enough to tie me down or hang me to a tree of death. Long ago I took God's promise made to my fathers and broke the shackles of despair. We go forth to make the world safe for democracy. After that job is well done we will make the United States safe for the Negro."[59]

Despite the apparent gains, blacks in some respects faced more formidable odds in 1913 than in 1863. Once a symbol of sectional strife, the Negro, within a span of fifty years, had become a symbol of national reconciliation based on the mutual embrace of white supremacy, a symbol around which white Northerners and Southerners could rally with equal conviction. The *Crisis*, the organ of the National Association for the Advancement of Colored People (NAACP; founded in 1909), used the occasion of the semicentennial of emancipation to provide a bleak assessment of the formidable barriers Southern blacks still confronted after fifty years of "attempted liberty": massive disfranchisement, widespread segregation, limited vocational education (which ensured a pool of servants and laborers), the subjugation of black women, and the eviction of blacks from the land by "disease, starvation or mob violence." Legislatures, courts of justice, the press, and secret societies lent their full support to this effort, as did an "acquiescent North." Against these odds, W. E. B. Du Bois urged his people to challenge white repression by mobilization and relentless agitation. "Abraham Lincoln began the emancipation of the Negro-American. The National Association for the Advancement of Colored People proposes to complete it."[60]

President Wilson made no mention in his inaugural address of the anniversary of emancipation or of the sixty black Southerners lynched in 1912, underscoring his and the nation's indifference to the reign of terror in the South. Four years later, when Wilson mobilized the nation to defend "the rights of all people," a black school principal in Alabama thought to ask, "Are we to share in the democracy for which we are now giving our lives? When the world is made safe for democracy, will the entire country be made safe for it?"[61] Throughout and after World War I, such questions persisted. "If a country can fight for democracy 3,000 miles across the sea," asked a black physician who had been forcibly expelled from his Mississippi community for disloyalty, "why [can] not simple justice be done at home?" In 1917, the year the president asked Congress to declare war, forty-six black Southerners lost their lives to lynch mobs. Before boarding trains bound for military camps, black recruits from Oklahoma reminded onlookers of what they were leaving behind, hoisting banners that read "Do Not Lynch Our Relatives While We Are Gone."[62]

Not all blacks embraced President Wilson's proclaimed mission, and some had little idea of why the United States had involved itself in a European conflict between equally oppressive colonial empires. Residing in a state where a black man had been lynched in 1917 for "seditious utterances," a black South Carolinian questioned the relevance of the war to his own life and condition. After all, he observed, "The Germans has not done us any harm and they cannot treat us any meaner than you all has." And he posted an ominous warning to white Americans, "Beware when you train 50,000 or 60,000 of the Negro race." That warning would be heard on numerous occasions during the war, repeated by whites and blacks alike. Training uniformed black men to kill whites might have dire consequences. "You low-down Mother Fuckers can put a gun in our hands but who is able to take it out?" asked Private Sidney Wilson, addressing the question to the chairman of his draft board in Tennessee and to a white Memphis newspaper. "We may go to France but I want to let you know that it will not be over with until we straiten up this state. We feel like we have nothing to do with this war, so if you all thinks it, just wait until Uncle Sam puts a gun in the niggers hands and you will be sorry of it, because we is sho goin to come back and fight and whip out the United States. . . . So all we wants now is the amanation [ammunition], then you all can look out, for we is coming."[63]

The contradictions were self-evident. Once again, as in the Civil War and the Spanish-American War, blacks were expected to respond favorably to the call to take up arms and defend abroad the rights that were denied to them at home. Some 370,000 black men became part of a segregated army, mostly assigned to labor battalions. (This restriction would help to allay whites' fears of blacks killing whites.) An adaptation of an old Negro spiritual repeated a timeless theme in blacks' experience with American wars: "'Twas the white man's fight, but the black man heard, / and went without a questioning word."[64] For the many who volunteered to serve, the reasons varied—from the chance to prove themselves worthy of citizenship to the opportunity to change their lives, see new lands, and work at jobs that rewarded them for their labor. A group of sawmill workers in North Carolina planned to break with the past by joining the army, and suggested a bluesy epitaph for their tombstone if they should be killed.

> Born in North Carolina
> Raised in Tennessee
> Worked like Hell in Georgia
> Died in Germinie.[65]

Among many blacks, the language of support rarely wavered: this was an opportunity to affirm their loyalty and patriotism. The Civil War had ended slavery, and the Great War (World War I), a black clergyman assured his people, would be a "second emancipation." After all, the NAACP declared, "if thousands of black men do fight in this world war, then who can hold from them the freedom that should be theirs in the end?"[66] Community leaders and organizations, churches, newspapers, and fraternal lodges played on this theme, urging their people to set aside doubts and mobilize in support of the war effort. A leading bishop in the African Methodist Episcopal (AME) church thought it important to advise his pastors to explain the draft to their congregations. "In this crisis in our American history, we should forget our creeds, classes, colors, and conditions, and stand out for Americanism—unsullied, untrammeled, and undismayed."[67] No one in black America articulated that sentiment more clearly or compellingly than W. E. B. Du Bois. "If this is OUR country," he insisted, "then this is OUR war." In his editorials for the *Crisis*, Du Bois urged his people to forget their "special grievances" and "close ranks . . . , shoulder to shoulder with our own white fellow citizens and the allied nations that are fighting for democracy. We make no ordinary sacrifice, but we make it gladly and willingly with our eyes lifted to the hills."[68]

But Du Bois's call to arms met with a mixed response in black America, failing to win the unanimity envisioned by either Du Bois or Wilson. Doubts about Negro morale and loyalty gave rise to growing concern. Upon the death of Booker T. Washington in 1915, Robert Russa Moton succeeded him as director of Tuskegee Institute. As an advisor to Wilson on racial policies, Moton traveled through the South in 1918 and reported to the president in a confidential letter that recent lynchings and burnings (including a six-person lynching in Georgia) had resulted in "more genuine restlessness and dissatisfaction on the part of the colored people than I have before known." Unless something was done, he warned, blacks were liable to become "indifferent or antagonistic" or "quietly hostile."[69] The following year, after visiting Tennessee and Mississippi, an NAACP official thought that "bloody conflicts impended in a number of southern cities."[70]

Much like whites who questioned or opposed the war,

black dissenters found themselves the victims of a hysteria that knew few if any restraints. For "circulating false reports," a black Arkansan was ordered to leave his community and warned that the "tree on which a negro was hanged several months ago is still standing."[71] In identifying alleged subversives who threatened the war effort, perhaps by refusing to buy any or enough Liberty Bonds, white vigilantes singled out—once again—the more successful and influential blacks. In Vicksburg, Mississippi, a respectable black physician, who had practiced medicine for eighteen years, was charged with "sedition," tarred and feathered, paraded through town, jailed, and banished under threat of death. That same day, vigilantes singled out three other blacks, accused them of disloyalty, expelled them from the community, and forced them to sell their property at a considerable loss. All of them belonged to the local black elite (a dentist, a pharmacist, and an attorney). It remains uncertain which factors played the largest role in determining the fate of these men: their leading role in organizing Mississippi's first NAACP branch or the fact that they were successful, well-educated black professionals—blacks out of their place.[72]

Regardless of the prevailing rhetoric about a war "to make the world safe for democracy," whites insisted on reinforcing the machinery of Jim Crow, making certain that military service in no way misled blacks about the proper relationship of the races. The humiliations and insults meted out to black soldiers, the persistence of Jim Crow (cafés, saloons, hotels, and railroad restaurants turned them away), and the number of blacks, many of them still in uniform, forced off the streets, driven out of their homes and communities, and stripped of their military uniforms and medals suggested the extent to which the war had intensified racial tensions, raising blacks' expectations along with whites' fears. "You see," a black Natchez veteran discovered soon after he returned home, "they [whites] are afraid that if the Negro kept up his idea of his being a soldier and fighting, and wearing guns, etc., that these Negroes wouldn't stand for all the insults which they have to take from white people."[73] If black men learned the "fighting game," one black leader asserted, they will not be so "aisily lynched."[74] The hostility black soldiers encountered in public was not surprising. White Southerners' antipathy to blacks in military uniform dated back to the Civil War, Union occupation, and Reconstruction. But the harassment and humiliation they had to endure in a segregated army was difficult to bear, along with the patriotic and religious hype that accompanied it.

What do the Generals and the Colonels do,
    I'll tell you—I'll tell you.
Figure out just how the privates ought to do
    The dirty little jobs for Jesus.

Fifty thousand privates died for Democracy,
    Dirty little job for Jesus,
Twenty Major Generals for the D.S.C.,
    Another dirty little job for Jesus.[75]

Shortly after the armistice that ended the war in 1918, James Weldon Johnson, who had earlier migrated to the

North from Florida and assumed the position of field secretary for the NAACP, recalled the day black recruits had marched to war carrying a flag stained with disfranchisement, Jim Crow, mob violence, and lynching. "The record of black men on the fields of France gives us the greater right to point to that flag and say to the nation: Those stains are still upon it; they dim its stars and soil its stripes; wash them out! wash them out!"[76]

Having urged blacks to "close ranks," a chastened Du Bois could only agree with Johnson's sense of betrayal. By May 1919, he was sounding a very different note.

> We sing: This country of ours, despite all its better souls have done and dreamed, is yet a shameful land.
>
> It *lynches*. . . .
>
> It *disfranchises* its own citizens. . . .
>
> It encourages *ignorance*. . . .
>
> It *steals* from us. . . .
>
> It *insults* us. . . .
>
> This is the country to which we Soldiers of Democracy return, This is the fatherland for *which* we fought! But it is *our* fatherland. . . .
>
> We *return*.
>
> We return from fighting.
>
> We return fighting.
>
> Make way for Democracy! We saved it in France, and by the Great Jehovah, we will save it in the United States of America, or know the reason why.[77]

In that same spirit, more than one observer of black America made a similar assessment of the black mood. "It [the war] has awakened race consciousness as never before."[78] Such a heightened black consciousness would be manifested in a variety of ways. During the war, it had drawn the attention not only of the federal government and military intelligence but of whites fearful of any changes in race relations. Whatever the patriotic hype and democratic rhetoric, the Great War did not force upon the nation the need to reexamine its dismal racial history. Black soldiers returned to an all too familiar America. Twenty veterans were among the seventy-seven Southern blacks lynched in 1919.[79] Still more—a far larger number, many still in uniform—were beaten and driven from their homes in many parts of the South. And in 1919 some four hundred blacks and whites were killed in twenty-five separate racial clashes and seven major race wars.

Whether before, during, or soon after the war, when whites took to the streets—as in Wilmington, North Carolina, in 1898, in Atlanta in 1906, in East St. Louis in 1916, in Chicago in 1919, or in Tulsa in 1921—they vented their exasperation over increasing evidence of blacks' aggressiveness, ambition, and disregard for racial etiquette. Journalists, politicians, and historians defined the outbursts as "race riots." But this term tends to obscure and distort what happened; more often than not, they were massacres, not riots. Whites terrorists lynched, murdered, assaulted, and plundered black residents, driving many of them into exile.

The principal targets were individuals, homes, and businesses that most vividly signified blacks "out of place" (trying to be white), and invariably these included leading and propertied blacks, those who had kept their faith in Booker T. Washington's uplift ideology—the most industrious, the most respectable, the most law-abiding, the most highly educated. In the 1921 Tulsa massacre, for example, a mob of ten thousand whites, sustained and protected (many of them deputized) by state and local law enforcement officers, singled out the section known as Greenwood or Little Africa, an enterprising and affluent community dubbed by some "the Negro Wall Street"—the home of black banks, businesses, law offices, schools, hotels, and theaters. Shaken by examples of black enterprise, the behavior of black war veterans, rumors (later disproved) of the attempted rape of a white woman, and reports that blacks were arming themselves to protect the suspect from a lynching, whites looted and leveled Greenwood.

In perhaps the costliest outbreak of racial violence in American history, as many as 150 to 200 people are said to have been killed, 90 percent of them black, some of them burned alive or tied to cars and dragged to death. Before the surging mobs withdrew, twenty-three churches, more than a thousand homes and businesses, and thirty-five city blocks were destroyed. There was talk among some whites of restitution, even of rebuilding the community, but it remained talk and empty promises; city officials, in fact, blocked efforts to reconstruct Greenwood. Blacks who had lost their property obtained no relief, and not a single person was charged with the deaths or the fires. "Following the great holocaust," recalled one survivor, Burt Colbert Franklin, "there was a great letdown in faith, ambition, hope, and trust." Nearly half a century later, a black journalist listened in disbelief to testimony about a riot most Tulsa whites preferred to forget. "Blacks lost everything, and they're afraid it could happen again," he wrote. "The killers are still running loose, and they're wearing blue suits as well as Klan sheets."[80]

Like Radical Reconstruction, the Great War permitted many black Americans—soldiers, factory workers, and migrants, for example—to glimpse other possibilities for their lives, and some managed to hold on to the wartime idealism that had initially raised their expectations. For those who had served overseas, however, travel underscored the provincialism of a segregated society at home. They found it difficult to return to an all too familiar South. Men and women who now worked in better-paying wartime jobs had no desire to return to menial labor or sharecropping. If they seemed restless, as some whites observed, if they were impatient, as some whites feared, it was because the war had promised so much and had delivered so little. The same Jim Crow signs screamed at them, the same racial etiquette humiliated them, the same schools educated them in separate and inferior facilities, and a heightened violence threatened them if they violated any precept of the racial code. The situation seemed largely unchanged, except for an increasingly restive black population and an increasingly wary and hostile white population. Some decades later, seeking the origins of the modern Civil Rights Movement, the retired president of Jackson College in Mississippi thought that the movement had gotten its start in

World War I—an important factor being the black soldier who had returned with a very different perspective on his native South. "He got the idea in World War I that he was a citizen, fighting for the country just as anyone else. . . . I think the return of the soldier after World War I was really the . . . beginning."[81]

That "beginning," however, would span four decades, during which the essential mechanisms, attitudes, and assumptions governing race relations in the South remained largely inviolate. Sporadic breakthroughs were made by individual blacks; the New Deal encouraged a politics of hope; and black men and women, collectively and individually, tested the limits of permissible dissent in an attempt to define their own place and future. The NAACP grew rapidly, and a reinvigorated labor movement, fed by organizing drives launched by the newly created Congress of Industrial Organizations (CIO), established beachheads of possibility in an industrializing South. But the mass of blacks still lived out their lives in a severely segregated, repressive, relatively static world. If the war had raised their expectations, the present and future, as bluesman Willie Brown suggested, offered little comfort:

Can't tell my future, I can't tell my past.
Lord, it seems like every minute sure gon' be my last.
Oh, minutes seems like hours, and hours seem like days.
Yes, minutes seems like hours, hours seems like days.[82]

On the eve of World War II, pondering what he had endured in his lifetime, Arthur Brodie, who lived in

Franklin County, North Carolina, felt numbed by the experience. "There's been so many times that you get to the point you feel it's a way of life for a long, long time."[83] No wonder that with the outbreak of World War II, the cynicism ran so deep in the black South. The same President Franklin Delano Roosevelt who told the Western democracies, "We Americans are vitally concerned in the defense of your freedom," placed a low priority on defending the freedom of black men and women in the United States. More than a million black Americans fought in World War II, as they had in World War I, to make the world safe for democracy. "What I wants to know," a young black man from Georgia thought to ask in 1942, "is, if democracy's so good for white folks, why ain't it good for niggers too."[84] The consciousness of black Americans, along with the struggle for black freedom, was about to be raised to new levels. "White folks talking about the Four Freedoms, and we ain't got none."[85] Some six weeks after Pearl Harbor, Cleo Wright, a black millworker, was lynched in Sikeston, Missouri. It took little time for black America to find and to invoke its battle cry for the duration of the war: "Remember Pearl Harbor—and Sikeston, Missouri."[86]

2 | Never Turn Back

Negroes, sweet and docile
Meek, humble, and kind:
Beware the day
They change their mind!

Wind
In the cotton fields,
Gentle breeze:
Beware the hour
It uproots trees!

> —Langston Hughes, "Warning" (1942)

The threats to the nation were "first Negroes, second Japs, third Nazis"—in just that order!

> —U.S. military officer in the Morale Division, drawing on letters and reports he had received during World War II[1]

On a Saturday night in November 1925, seventeen-year-old Richard Wright packed his suitcase, said goodbye to his mother, and left his native Mississippi, fleeing "that most racist of all the American states." Fifteen years later, in the summer of 1940, he returned to visit relatives and to ascertain how much the South had changed. "I'm going to risk it," he told a worried friend. As soon as the train entered the South, Wright had to move to a separate railroad coach and no longer had access to the dining car. Whites addressed him as "boy" and "nigger," and they eyed suspiciously the typewriter he was carrying. When he explained to one white man that he was a writer, the man was clearly baffled and asked Wright where he'd been born. "Mississippi," Wright replied. That brought a knowing smile to the white man's face. "I knew you was a southern nigger. You niggers can travel all over the world, but when I see a southern nigger, I know it." That ended the conversation, and the relieved white man walked away.

On returning to the South, Wright was greeted by the same old signs that read "White" and "Colored." The shacks in which the sharecroppers and laborers lived stood upon the red clay, baking in the hot sun. In the towns, the narrow alleys gave off all too familiar smells, the cooking odors and the stench of outdoor privies mixing with the sweet scent of magnolias. In the evenings and on Sunday afternoons, the town Negroes and field laborers gathered in the taverns, as they had in Wright's youth, and invariably the conversations turned to swapping stories about white folks, stories that "would whip them to bitter laughter."

The spot where Wright had been born was now a jungly tangle of weeds and trees; the house had burned to the ground, as there had been no water to douse the flames when it had caught fire. He learned that the local schools still offered few if any opportunities for black children to improve their knowledge or their lives. During his brief stay, Wright witnessed no violence and no lynchings, only "the normal routine of daily relations between Negroes and whites." That was enough to satisfy his curiosity; indeed, the first two hours told him everything he needed to know. "Jim Crow was still Jim Crow, and not a single racial practice had altered during my absence. What I saw made me wonder why I had wanted to see and feel it all again. I discovered that the only thing that had really changed was I."[2]

For most blacks, in the years just before World War II the South remained quite familiar. Jim Crow was alive and well. The narrow boundaries, the limited options, the need to curb ambitions, to contain feelings, to weigh carefully every word, gesture, and movement when in the presence of whites—all these constraints still shaped black lives. Personal security lay in repressing any impulses toward individuality or assertiveness, in learning how to accommodate to daily indignities. Three-fourths of adult blacks had not finished high school; some nine out of ten families lived below the federal poverty threshold; blacks earned about 39 percent of what whites made. Fewer than 5 percent of eligible blacks in the old Confederacy could exercise the right to vote.

It was from this vantage point that black Southerners viewed the events unfolding in Europe and Asia. Four days before the United States entered the war, Charles Jenkins wrote to President Roosevelt: "If there is such a thing as God, he must be a white person, according to the conditions we colored people are in. Hitler has not done anything to the colored people—it's the people right here in the United States who are keeping us out of work and keeping us down."[3] The cynicism was rooted in the conviction that this was a white man's war, involving colonial nations—such as France and Great Britain—that had a sordid record of racist repression and exploitation in their respective empires.

Even after Pearl Harbor and America's entry into the war, the mood of cynicism did not suddenly evaporate in a patriotic frenzy. Many blacks remained indifferent; some could no longer contain the rage and resentment they felt. "I hope Hitler does come," a black domestic in Raleigh, North Carolina, told her employer, "because if he does he will get you first!" (She was sentenced to three years in prison for her outburst.)[4] For some, however, the war seemed distant and much less important than the daily struggle for survival. Unable to enjoy the rights and privileges accorded white Americans, blacks might well have wondered if it was indeed *their* country that was under attack. An old black sharecropper, after coming to the Big House to receive his ration of cornmeal and fatback from the plantation owner, noted in passing the news of Pearl Harbor. "By the way Captain, I hear the Japs done declared war on you white folks!"[5] At a loss to understand what the war was all about, a small black community in the backwoods of Mississippi finally decided to send someone to a nearby town to get answers. Trying to be as unobtrusive as possible, he picked up some scattered references to the rape of Hawaii, and reported to his community that Uncle Sam and the Japanese were fighting about an "old whore" called Pearl Harbor.[6]

As the war progressed the issues became clearer, but for many blacks the questions about the war's meaning and implications grew more insistent. How could white Americans express outrage over the plight of Jews while remaining indifferent to the lynching and brutalization of black Americans? How could a Jim Crow army fight for a free world? How could black Americans fight abroad in defense of freedoms denied to them at home? No amount of patriotic hype could settle or postpone answers to these questions. "The Negro today is angry, resentful and utterly apathetic about the war," a black writer observed early in 1942. "'Fight for what?' he is asking. 'This war doesn't mean a thing to me. If we win I lose, so what?'"[7] The war slogans found no ready acceptance in black America. Private Charles Williams, stationed in Texas, had enlisted in the belief he would be fighting for a just cause. "I was glad to fight for the four freedoms. Now I am confused as to their meaning. I want to soldier. But I want to soldier as a man, not as a nigger." He vowed to remain A.W.O.L. until he was transferred to an outfit "where I can see the necessity of fighting."[8]

With the attack on Pearl Harbor, blacks responded to the calls for loyalty with a conditional patriotism. Rather than lessen the agitation for civil rights in the spirit of wartime unity, they would heighten their efforts. "So we must speak, even as we fight and die," proclaimed the *Crisis*, the organ of the NAACP.

We must say that the fight against Hitlerism begins in Washington, D.C., the capital of our nation, where black Americans have a status only slightly above that of Jews in Berlin. We must say that if forced labor is wrong in Czechoslovakia, peonage farms are wrong in Georgia. If the ghettos in Poland are an evil, so are the ghettos in America. We must say that the enslavement of the bodies and spirits of men, of whatever color, or race, or residence, must be wiped out. We must say all the things that cry aloud to be said—not later, but now.[9]

This theme persisted throughout the war. If blacks did not agitate for their rights now, when the government depended on their loyalty and services, it would be too late after the war.[10]

With unprecedented solidarity in the black populace, civil rights and community organizations, along with the black press and black churches, exposed and attacked the gross disparities between the American democratic creed, the announced aims of the war, and the nation's racial practices. Protest became not only widespread but respectable, involving individuals never before mobilized in the struggle for civil rights. Membership in the NAACP increased nearly tenfold, the number of chapters tripled, and the membership crossed class lines, becoming more representative of the black population, increasing the organization's reach, and altering its strategies and direction. The black press also played a critical role, despite attempts at censorship and threats to deprive it of necessary but scarce newsprint. Black newspapers maintained their vigilance, covering in depth every racial incident and every reported invasion of civil rights.[11] Public officials expressed concern that black news coverage might fragment the nation's wartime unity, but their statements had little effect. By May 1942, the influential *Pittsburgh Courier*, with an impressive readership outside the city, found the "hysteria" in Washington, D.C., over black morale "an astonishing, amusing and shameful spectacle. . . . Squelching the Negro newspapers will not make the Negro masses love insult, discrimination, exploitation and ostracism. It will only further depress their morale."[12]

If most blacks accepted, with varying degrees of enthusiasm, their obligation to serve in the military, and if some believed (as had blacks in previous wars) that their service would be recognized, respected, and honored and would alter white attitudes, many retained their doubts and concerns upon receiving their registration materials.

> I was sittin' here wonderin' with my number, in that
> old goldfish bowl,
> I was sittin' here wonderin' with my number, in that
> old goldfish bowl,
> An' when I heard my number called, oooh Lord, I
> couldn't feel happy to save my soul.[13]

This time, perhaps mindful of how they had "closed ranks" in the mobilization for World War I, blacks responded with less alacrity. This time the pessimism, the ambivalence, the bitterness, the frustration, the cynicism ran much deeper. For one young black man who was about to be inducted into the army, the very nature of the war and its racial implications tempered his enthusiasm and patriotism: "Just carve on my tombstone, 'Here lies a black man killed fighting a yellow man for the protection of a white man.'"[14]

For generations, black Southerners had used various ploys to capitalize on white expectations. Since many employers deemed them troublesome and unemployable, they would play to those expectations and "make a career of natural badness," turning white rejection and stereotyping to their advantage. "A nigger is a nigger," they would say, "he lives in the basement . . . no use to run upstairs." In the 1930s, a black songwriter would give voice to precisely this attitude.

'Cause white folks expect nigger to be lazy
Ain't no cause to worry
I wouldn't disappoints him for the world
That's why I never hurry.[15]

Some blacks adopted a similar strategy in World War II when they appeared at the induction center. Malcolm Little (Malcolm X) showed up at his physical as a Harlem jivester, wearing his most outrageous zoot suit and yellow shoes. He professed great enthusiasm for serving his country. "I want to get sent down South," he confided to the psychiatrist. "Organize them nigger soldiers, you dig? Steal us some guns, and kill up crackers!" The psychiatrist's blue pencil dropped, his professional manner suddenly evaporated, and he fumbled for his red pencil. "I knew I had him. . . . A 4-F card came to me in the mail, and I never heard from the Army any more, and never bothered to ask why I was rejected."[16]

If blacks needed "to fight for the right to fight for democracy," as Walter White of the NAACP insisted, some blacks could not muster sufficient enthusiasm for the war to make that kind of commitment. Eddie Boyd, a bluesman born in Mississippi, chose to work in defense plants to avoid military service. He migrated to Chicago in 1941, vowing to obtain employment "at the cheapest defense plant, where it was hard for them to keep labor." That, he recalled, set him apart from blacks "crazy enough" to want to fight. "I never saw this to be my fight. My war was here, you understand. That's the way I seen it, man. I want to be free. Who am I gonna fight for? Fight to help America win a war, and then that make him more powerful than before I went over there."[17] For John Hope Franklin, a native Oklahoman and a black teacher and scholar, military service raised serious questions about fighting abroad for rights denied to blacks at home. With a Ph.D. from Harvard and an impressive academic record, Franklin aspired to serve "in some capacity where my talents and my training could be fully utilized." But as one recruiting officer made clear, Franklin lacked one critical qualification: the right "color." After being rebuffed by the Department of War (which was organizing a group of historians to write the official history of the war) and rejected by the Navy (which confined blacks to menial positions), Franklin concluded that the United States neither needed nor deserved his services.[18]

To avoid military service, some blacks simply dropped out. That is, rather than adopting a deliberate strategy to avoid serving in the military, they showed up at the pre-induction examination and told the army psychiatrist how they felt about making such a commitment. "Man, why should I fight?" Howard McGhee asked the psychiatrist. "I ain't mad at nobody out there. . . . I wouldn't know the difference. . . . If he's white, I'm going to shoot him. Whether he's a Frenchman, a German, or whatever, how the fuck would I know the difference?" The army informed McGhee it could not use his services. "I wasn't ready to dodge no bullets for nobody," McGhee later reflected. "And I like America. But I didn't like it that much. I mean, it's all right to be a second-class citizen, but shit, to be shot at, that's another damn story.[19] Dizzy Gillespie attracted the attention of the army psychiatrist when he appeared carrying his trumpet in a paper bag. His words attracted even more attention.

> They started asking me my views about fighting. "Well, look, at this time, in this stage of my life here in the United States, whose foot has been in my ass? The white man's foot has been in my ass hole, buried up to his knee in my ass hole! Now, you're speaking of the enemy. You're telling me the German is the enemy. At this point, I can never even remember having met a German. So if you put me out there with a gun in my hand and tell me to shoot at the enemy, I'm liable to create a case of 'mistaken identity,' of who I might shoot." . . . They finally classified me 4F because I was crazy enough not to want to fight in anybody's army.[20]

When Willie Dixon was drafted, he ignored the summons and was arrested and tried. Born in Vicksburg,

Mississippi, in 1915, he had migrated to Chicago as a teenager, escaping from a prison farm to which he had been sent for "hoboing." When the war broke out, he was "involved in music," writing and playing blues. During his trials, he affirmed his unwillingness to serve ("I made up my mind I wasn't going no damn where"), and he remained unrepentant. "I didn't feel I had to go because of the conditions that existed among my people. . . . I explained to them in several court cases, 'Why should I go to work to fight to save somebody what's killing me and my people?' I said I wasn't a citizen, I was a subject." When reminded that he had been born in the United States, Dixon replied, "Hell, that doesn't make you anything. All my folks were born here. . . . An egg can be hatched in a stove but that doesn't make it a biscuit just because it came out of the stove." Every time he appeared in court he reminded the judge of the workings of Jim Crow, creating "such a helluva commotion . . . they were afraid to let me out and afraid to leave me in jail because they said I was influencing the black people's mind about going into the army." Finally, he was fined, sentenced, and released, reclassified a 5-F. "I don't know what that meant and nobody else did, either." He never knew why they had released him. "I guess they must have felt like I would be better off for them on the outside because I'd have to hustle like hell for a living."[21]

To quantify black reactions to military service and the war would be impossible. Polls were notoriously unreliable, as blacks invariably knew from experience to tell the white man what they thought the white man wanted to hear. Still, there is substantial reason to believe that in the streets and rural crossroads of black America many people shared the cynicism and evinced the same spirit that motivated McGhee, Gillespie, and Dixon. Wherever black men and women gathered, the subject of the war provoked considerable discussion, as Enoch Waters Jr., a reporter for the black newspaper *Chicago Defender*, observed:

> The men in the barbershop, on the assembly line, sweeping the floors or washing windows know their spirit concerning the war is not right. They can't diagnose it. Uncle Sam is aware of it too, and he calls it morale. So the millions of Negroes who go through all the motions of patriotism—and are actually patriotic— do not feel patriotic, because in the recesses of their minds there is disturbance, a disturbance which won't quiet.[22]

That "disturbance" was articulated in various ways, but the theme that would be repeated time and again focused on the unfairness implicit in asking black men to enlist in a Jim Crow army to fight for a nation that showed no signs of diminishing the humiliation and discrimination inflicted on black people. While waiting for a bus in downtown Nashville, a black mother with two sons in the army expressed dismay over the attitudes and behavior of whites. "To think that our boys are fighting and then they don't want to recognize us makes a mother who has stood in the white folks' kitchen trying to put her children through school feel mighty bad sometimes." That same questioning spirit induced a black soldier in

New Orleans to refuse a bus driver's order to sit in the Jim Crow section. "They tell me I'm supposed to fight for democracy," he explained to the driver. "I may as well start here."[23]

Similar reports of uneasiness surfaced throughout the country (many of them recorded by military intelligence); they were by no means confined to the South. In Harlem, a white draft board member had been accustomed to giving black draftees "a little patriotic talk to make them feel good." It didn't, he confessed. "They only laughed at me. Now I bow my head as they come in for their induction."[24]

Although blacks were familiar with the racist doctrines of Nazi Germany, they tended to be more ambivalent about Japan. If asked, many blacks took pains to flaunt their loyalty and denied knowing of any pro-Japanese feeling based on color. Others, however, agreed that even if blacks did not manifest pro-Japanese sentiments, some took vicarious pleasure during the early months of the war in seeing white America humbled, if not humiliated. "If them Japs can give these white people a good beating," a black "man on the street" observed, "it will be good for all the colored people."[25] Some speculated that "white folks are jumping on the nigger" because they were "downright scared" of the Japanese. "These Japs really got them worried, and I hope they beat them good."[26]

If nothing else, Japanese successes deflated notions of white supremacy. A black schoolteacher in rural North Carolina, while making it clear she did not prefer or like the Japanese way of life, nonetheless admired the fact that Japan was "demanding," not "requesting or begging," and that it dared to challenge a white nation. "I've been so used to pulling for the underdogs, until I all but root for the Japs." But realizing that such a view was "dangerous," she would tell whites what she knew they wanted to hear. "I allow myself to resent them [the Japanese] for my protection."[27] In defending a black worker arrested for telling a white man, "The Japs will settle with you for this," a black minister in Birmingham understood that "like a lot of young men," if this soldier "was going off to fight for democracy, he might as well get a last fling and stand up for his rights before going." At the same time, the minister admonished his people, "We've got to learn to keep our mouths shut in front of white people about the war."[28]

Tolbert Chism, an Arkansas black who traced his ancestry to the Choctaw Indians, provided a unique perspective when he heard news of the fall of the Philippines and the infamous Bataan Death March, in which Japanese soldiers brutalized U.S. prisoners-of-war. He thought it a long-delayed "payback" for America's mistreatment of the Indians more than a century earlier. The Death March reminded him of the Trail of Tears, the forced march of Indians to the Oklahoma Territory in which thousands of Choctaws lost their lives. "Many people aren't aware of that, never did even give that a thought. Something greater than ourselves intervened and kind of gave those who were in power kind of payback for what they had done in the past."[29]

Whatever these stories suggest about the depths of black disillusionment, the threat of Hitlerism and Nazi racial theories was not lost on black Americans. The outbreak of World War II found most of them responding (once again) to the call to defend their country and help make the world safe for democracy. If some blacks expressed cynicism about the democratic slogans, others kept the faith. A war to wipe out Nazi bigotry promised to eradicate racist bigotry in the United States. As in previous wars, blacks argued that a display of patriotism and military service would be rewarded; it would lay the basis for a new compact with whites after the war. Although the Double V slogan (victory over enemies abroad and victory over racial repression at home) helped to mobilize blacks behind the war effort, a black domestic thought to advise her people not to be slackers. "Negroes should fight just like everybody else; it's their home, too, they are defending. . . . That 'V' at home won't do us a bit of good if we lose that 'V' abroad."[30]

Most blacks managed to serve credibly and loyally, and many of them had few illusions that the war would make any significant difference in their lives. Wilson Evans had experienced segregation and police harassment while growing up in Gulfport, Mississippi, and he was less than patriotic when the war broke out. "I figured if the Japs took America that I would fare better. . . . I didn't know at that time all that I know now about Hitler." Nonetheless, he thought it unlikely that Hitler could match a Mississippi policeman in meanness. After he was drafted and made his way across Europe as an infantryman, fighting in the Battle of the Bulge, he still questioned the differences (if any) between Nazi racism and American racism. Once he realized that the Nazis had no interest in his mother's home in Mississippi, he expressed relief. "They wanted downtown Gulfport and all, and as far as I was concerned, hell, they could have it."[31]

The variation in black responses persisted throughout the war. To a black soldier stationed in England, the alternatives were quite clear. "I am fighting to kill Germans before we are all made slaves."[32] Still another GI, a Floridian, claimed he was fighting "to be free from segregation."[33] Bluesman Sonny Boy Williamson was downright ecstatic about performing his patriotic duty.

> I want to drop a bomb, and set the Japanese city
>   on fire,
> I want to drop a bomb, and set the Japanese city on
>   fire,
> Now because they are so rotten, I just love to see
>   them die.
>
> I've got the Victory Blues because I know I've got
>   to go,
> I've got the Victory Blues because I know I've got
>   to go,
> Now to keep the Japanese from slipping in through
>   my baby's back door.[34]

Reflecting on his war experience, a Southern black farmer could name no ideological cause for which he had fought. He'd simply fought to survive. And this opinion seemed more representative of black (and much of white) thinking than any other: "I was trying to live. I had to fight to live to get back home. I didn't have any principle. I was there because I was drafted. I felt that the only way I'm going to survive to get back is to learn how to shoot good and ask questions later."[35]

The response that resonated with many black Americans was that they fought because they preferred a flawed United States to a Nazi-controlled Germany. Heavyweight champion Joe Louis, the hero of black America, articulated this sentiment when he declared, "There may be a whole lot wrong with America, but there's nothing that Hitler can fix." Several years earlier, Louis had defeated Max Schmeling of Germany in a boxing showdown of international significance. Schmeling symbolized Hitler's doctrine of Aryan superiority. Upon Joe Louis, then, fell the responsibility for upholding America's pride and the democratic way of life. "Joe, we're depending on those muscles for America," President Roosevelt reminded him. Almost all Americans were pulling for him, Louis later recalled. "White Americans—even while some of them still were lynching black people in the South—were depending on me to K.O. Germany." Novelist Richard Wright, who had also come to national attention with the publication of *Native Son* in 1940, composed lyrics which Count Basie later set to music and which became the song "King Joe." "Wonder what Joe Louis thinks when he's fighting a white man / Bet he thinks what I'm thinking 'cause he wears a deadpan." Louis knocked out Schmeling in the first round, but he would enter the army a black American.

"They gave me my uniform, and sent me over to the colored section."[36]

For many blacks, military service afforded them not only a chance to demonstrate their patriotism but the rare opportunity to escape the economic and social subordination that circumscribed their lives as civilians. Bluesman Arthur "Big Boy" Crudup glimpsed still another option that military service made possible: a chance to commit murder within the law.

> I've got my questionairy and they need me in the war
> I've got my questionairy and they need me in the war
> Now if I feel like murder, won't have to break the
>   county law.
>
> All I want is a 32-20, made on a .45 frame,
> All I want is a 32-20, made on a .45 frame,
> Yes, and a red, white, and blue flag waving in my right
>   hand.
>
> Now if I go down, with a red, white and blue flag in
>   ma hand,
> Now if I go down, with a red, white and blue flag in
>   ma hand,
> Say, you can bet your life poor Crudup sent many a
>   man.[37]

What Crudup envisioned, white Southerners feared. No matter how hard they tried, whites found no way to resolve their ambivalence about black military service. They had to weigh their traditional fear of blacks in uniform against their fears of what might happen if more white males departed for the war, leaving their womenfolk behind. (Nazi propagandists exploited this issue at

the front, airdropping illustrated fliers that depicted naked white women—presumably the spouses or sweet-
hearts of white servicemen—in the arms of naked black
men.) The fact that many black men were rejected because they failed to pass literacy tests alarmed whites,
who were now paying a price for "enforced illiteracy"—
that is, for generations of neglect of black education.
Southern congressmen, no doubt reflecting the concerns
of their constituents, called attention to the disproportionate number of white inductees and demanded that
blacks be drafted in sufficient numbers to replace those
who were rejected.[38]

As in the Civil War, some blacks believed that only a
prolonged conflict would enable them to achieve their
objectives at home. The longer the war, the more they
might make of their opportunities, turning white depen-
dence on their loyalty into measurable gains. "Not only
will a long war develop a new white outlook," one black
columnist wrote, "but a new black outlook as well.
. . . America will need the Negro as never before and will
act accordingly. Let the struggle last for many years and
there will be interracially little resemblance left to the
United States of December 7, 1941."[39] The fact that
black military units were eventually sent into combat has
been attributed to the length of the war and to wartime
needs, as well as to relentless black pressure. During the
course of the war the armed services moved from exclusion (as in the Marines and Air Corps) and confinement
to menial duty (as in the Navy) to segregation and finally
to sporadic attempts at integration.[40]

Black servicemen underwent basic training in segregated camps, mostly in the South, before being assigned to menial or construction labor. This was their "place" in the armed forces—the same place they occupied in civilian life. And this was where most Americans expected them to stay. But as in the Civil War, that position was bound to fluctuate with the progress made on the battle fronts.

> Well, airplanes flyin' 'cross the land and the sea,
> Everybody flyin' but a Negro like me.
> Uncle Sam says, "Your place is on the ground,
> When I fly my airplanes, don't want no Negro
>   'round."
>
> The same thing for the navy, ships goes to sea,
> All they got is a mess boy's job for me.
> Uncle Sam says, "Keep on your apron, son,
> You know I ain't gonna let you shoot my big navy
>   gun."
>
> Got my long government letters, my time to go,
> When I got to the army, found the same old Jim
>   Crow.
> Uncle Sam says, "Two camps for black and white,"
> But when trouble starts, we'll all be in that same big
>   fight.[41]

Even before America's entrance into the war, blacks had questioned the obstacles they faced in serving their country. Perhaps, in this context, Richard Wright's memorable creation Bigger Thomas most cogently addressed the fears of whites in explaining why blacks should not aspire to get out of their place, even in defense of their country under attack from a foreign enemy. In the opening scene of *Native Son*, Bigger Thomas and his friend Gus watch a plane fly overhead. "Them white boys sure can fly," Gus remarks, to which Bigger responds, "I could fly one of them things if I had a chance."

> Gus pulled down the corners of his lips, stepped out from the wall, squared his shoulders, doffed his cap, bowed low and spoke with mock deference:
> "Yessuh."
> "You go to hell," Bigger said, smiling.
> "Yessuh," Gus said again.
> "I could fly a plane if I had a chance," Bigger said.
> "If you wasn't black and if you had some money and if they'd let you go to that aviation school, you could fly a plane," Gus said.
> For a moment Bigger contemplated all the "ifs" that Gus had mentioned. Then both boys broke into hard laughter, looking at each other through squinted eyes. When their laughter subsided, Bigger said in a voice that was half-question and half-statement:
> "It's funny how the white folks treat us, ain't it?"
> "It better be funny," Gus said.
> "Maybe they right in not wanting us to fly," Bigger said. "Cause if I took a plane up I'd take a couple of bombs along and drop 'em as sure as hell."[42]

The U.S. Air Force in 1940 claimed it excluded blacks not out of a fear that black pilots might choose to drop bombs on the wrong targets, but because blacks were said to possess neither the intelligence required to perform the technical functions of a pilot nor the courage to fly airplanes in combat.

The outburst by Bigger Thomas, however, addressed a

much larger issue: the condition of black men and women in white America and their systematic exclusion from participation in the larger society. The struggle for "the right to fight for democracy" took on a special meaning with dire consequences for black aspirations. If denied the right to fight for their country on an equal basis with whites, what could blacks envision after the war but a return to the racial status quo? Black agitation focused on this question, and there was much to agitate about. The rigidly segregated army into which blacks were inducted reflected at all levels the belief that blacks were inferior to whites, whether in flying planes or handling firearms or assuming the responsibility of command. Secretary of War Henry Stimson vowed that the U.S. Army would not be turned into a "sociological laboratory." General George Marshall insisted that desegregation of the army violated American customs and would destroy morale. Both agreed that "leadership" was not "embedded in the negro race" and that segregated blacks had to serve under white officers (preferably Southerners, who allegedly knew how to handle and control them).[43]

Even as President Roosevelt committed the nation to a worldwide struggle for freedom, black soldiers faced a denial of that freedom, coupled with acts of discrimination, violence, and humiliation. "To be a black soldier in the South in those days was one of the worst things that could happen to you," testified Johnnie Stevens of the 761st Tank Battalion.

> If you go to town, you would have to get off the sidewalk if a white person came by. If you went into the

wrong neighborhood wearing your uniform, you got beat up. If you stumbled over a brick, you was drunk and got beat up. If off-post you was hungry and couldn't find a black restaurant or a black home you know, you know what? You would starve. And you were a soldier . . . out there wearing the uniform of your country, and you're getting treated like a dog! That happened all over the South.[44]

And it happened to black officers as well as recruits, many of them Northerners initiated into the workings of Jim Crow. If anything, with the number of Northern blacks present and fears raised over the conduct of Southern-born blacks, white vigilance mounted with every incident—every encroachment on the dominant racial etiquette, every verbal exchange with whites. One black officer, home on furlough from a Southern camp, tried his best to contain the rage he felt over his treatment. He did not want to talk about the war or his military service. While on leave, he wanted to get as far from the army as possible.

Sure I'm in it. But I hate it! I hate it because, above everything else in this country, the Army treats the Negro worst. I hate it because my own government won't protect me against any white man, in or out of the Army. I hate it because every day since I've been in the Army some white person has reminded me through some word or act that, although I wear the uniform of an officer of the United States Army, I'm still nothing but a "nigger." I've been in hundreds of bull sessions with other colored fellows and I have until yet to hear a single man express any loyalty for his own country.

What the hell do we want to fight the Japs for anyhow? They couldn't possibly treat us any worse than these "crackers" right here at home.[45]

The black press documented the abuses: the insults hurled at black GIs, the harassment by MPs, the hostility of civilians in towns near military bases, especially in the South, where Jim Crow laws were relentlessly enforced. Many black service members, including army nurses, were brutally beaten and jailed for defying Jim Crow laws; many more were simply turned away from hotels, restaurants, and taverns. Violent racial clashes, with a disproportionate number of black casualties, broke out at army bases in the South, many in the North and West, and some overseas. USO and service clubs, PXs, and canteens might exclude blacks on the nights white soldiers were admitted, or provide separate facilities, or bar black soldiers altogether. "It is pretty grim," observed an NAACP official, "to have a black boy in uniform get an orientation lecture in the morning on wiping out Nazi bigotry, and that same evening be told he can buy a soft drink only in the 'Colored' PX." Segregated chapels existed on many bases, and some found a unique way to post the schedule of religious services: "Catholic, Jews, Protestants and Negroes." The bases maintained segregated entertainment centers, and the Red Cross ordered that the blood plasma from white and black donors be kept separate. Any black soldier who questioned these practices ran the risk of transfer, imprisonment, or dishonorable discharge.[46]

The ultimate humiliation was best described by Lloyd Brown, when he recalled the greeting he and his fellow black soldiers received in Salina, Kansas when they entered a lunchroom on the main street:

As we entered, the counterman hurried to the rear to get the owner, who hurried out front to tell us with urgent politeness: "You boys know we don't serve colored here." Of course we knew it. They didn't serve "colored" anywhere in town. . . . The best movie house did not admit Negroes and the other one admitted them only to the balcony. There was no room at the inn for any black visitor, and there was no place in town where he could get a cup of coffee. "You know we don't serve colored here," the man repeated. . . . We ignored him, and just stood there inside the door, staring at what we had come to see—the German prisoners of war who were having lunch at the counter. There were about ten of them. . . . No guard was with them. . . . We continued to stare. This was really happening. It was no jive talk. It was the Gospel truth. The people of Salina would serve these enemy soldiers and turn away black American G.I.'s. . . . If we were untermenschen in Nazi Germany, they would break our bones. As "colored" men in Salina, they only break our hearts.[47]

What Lloyd Brown had seen was by no means rare. Nazi POWs en route to POW camps in the South and in parts of the Midwest and West were permitted to eat with white soldiers, guards, and civilians in railroad dining cars and in station restaurants, but black soldiers, even if assigned to guard the POWs, were barred from such facilities. This, to bluesman B. B. King, was an "eye-opener."

> German prisoners of war were on the same train. But unlike us, they weren't forced to sit in separate and inferior compartments. They sat with the white folk. And these were our sworn enemies! . . . It upset me even worse when I saw how the German prisoners were used to pick cotton in the Delta. We blacks picked till nightfall—seven or eight in the evening. But the Germans were allowed to take off at three in the afternoon. Plantation owners worried about overworking them. That made us feel less than human. We were seen as beasts of burden, dumb animals, a level below the Germans. To watch your enemy get better treatment than yourself was a helluva thing to endure. . . . As a kid, I was brainwashed by a segregated system. I was taught caution and strict adherence to society's codes. As a twenty-year-old, fresh out of basic training, I was starting to feel the weight of the system. I felt the injustice. And I felt anger.[48]

Matthew J. Perry of South Carolina had the same experience, watching Italian POWs sitting in a railroad terminal restaurant that barred blacks. "You have no idea the feeling of insult that I experienced." It helped persuade Perry to enter law school after the war; and he was soon propelled into the Civil Rights Movement and into the federal judiciary—South Carolina's first black U.S. District Court Judge. George Holloway worked as a Pullman porter on a train bringing German POWs from California to Mississippi. When they stopped in Little

Rock, the German prisoners ate in a beautiful chandeliered dining room. The porters ate in the kitchen. Newspapers made much of the incident, but one of Mississippi's senators had an immediate response to the uproar. "The Germans are white, aren't they?"[49]

At one prisoner-of-war camp, black entertainer Lena Horne appeared. The camp commander had filled the front rows with German POWs; their black guards had to sit in the back of the auditorium. "I don't think I have ever been more furious in my life," Lena Horne recalled. She stepped down from the stage, walked up the aisle, and with her back turned to the POWs sang to her own people in the back of the hall. "But by the third or fourth song I was too choked with anger and humiliation to go on." After the performance, she wired the USO that she was leaving the tour. "The word was very quietly passed down," she remembered, "to keep that big-mouth woman out of the Southern camps."[50]

For black soldiers to see and hear the likes of Lena Horne had to be a rare and welcome treat in an otherwise dreary procession of stereotyped Negroes portrayed on the screens of the segregated moviehouses. A major form of amusement and diversion for soldiers, movies fed the dominant racial stereotypes and were a source of embarrassment to blacks. One infantry soldier, writing a letter home, thought to express his disgust over what he was viewing. He singled out black women playing the role of illiterate maids and black men who act fearful, "stupid, dumb and ignorant" in the presence of whites, use an exaggerated drawl, and widen and roll their eyes. "It is difficult to fight for one's country," he declared, "with something like that going on." He ended his letter, nonetheless, on a note of racial affirmation. "I'm proud that I am a Negro, but I don't like to see my people act as if they were just in AMERICA to take up space."[51]

In the minds of white Southerners, the war posed grave challenges to the etiquette of race relations and to cherished customs and traditions that marked the "place" of blacks in the social order. To maintain that place became, during the war, a racial and patriotic necessity, defended as a war emergency and deemed essential to the morale of white soldiers, workers, and civilians. Under a large red "V for Victory" banner, this sign appeared in a Charleston, South Carolina, bus:

VICTORY DEMANDS YOUR COOPERATION. IF THE PEOPLES OF THIS COUNTRY'S RACES DO NOT PULL TOGETHER, VICTORY IS LOST. WE, THEREFORE, RESPECTFULLY DIRECT YOUR ATTENTION TO THE LAWS AND CUSTOMS OF THE STATE IN REGARD TO SEGREGATION. YOUR COOPERATION IN CARRYING THEM OUT WILL MAKE THE WAR SHORTER AND VICTORY SOONER. AVOID FRICTION. BE PATRIOTIC. WHITE PASSENGERS WILL BE SEATED FROM FRONT TO REAR; COLORED PASSENGERS FROM REAR TO FRONT.[52]

In Columbus, Georgia, buses flaunting the slogan, "K.O. for Tokyo" passed black soldiers waiting for special buses that would take them back to Fort Benning.[53]

If blacks expressed concern and outrage over fighting a war that would preserve white supremacy, whites articulated fears that their sons might be fighting a war that could threaten their supremacy. "There's no white man down here going to let his daughter sleep with a nigger, or sit at the same table with a nigger, or go walking with a nigger," warned a leader of the Birmingham Chamber of Commerce. "The war can go to hell, the world can go to hell, but he ain't going to do it."[54] Making good on that vow, whites maintained a rigorous watch over any breaches in racial etiquette, and the police and white vigilantes meted out the appropriate punishments, legal and extralegal. "I am afraid for my people," a black clergyman in North Carolina declared in 1943, anticipating a white backlash. "They have grown restless. They are not happy. They no longer laugh. There is a new feeling among them—something strange, perhaps terrible."[55]

As the Double V slogan suggested, World War II would be fought on two fronts. That is, blacks would moderate their patriotism and commitment to the war effort in accordance with facts on the ground—progress made on the racial front at home. When one black observer was asked if blacks supported the war, he replied, "The Negro is all out for it," but quickly qualified that view, "He's 72 percent all out for it." That estimate, he added, might reflect optimism for some, cynicism for others. But clearly, he concluded, "hardly to be disputed" was the fact that this war, "for all of its high promise, . . . has not summoned 100 percent of the Negro's enthusiasm and energies." Sterling Brown spent six months in

the South during the war. Among the blacks he met—
civilians and military men, upper-class and lower-class
people, conservatives and radicals—many expressed "a
sense of not belonging, and protest, sometimes not loud
but always deeply felt."[56] Throughout the war, that "new
feeling" among blacks, North and South, would be manifested in guerilla warfare aimed at the formidable structure of Jim Crow.

Although Jim Crow survived the war, challenges to its
legitimacy reached historic proportions, as black men
and women, usually without organization and as individuals, ignored segregation ordinances. Thousands of
black men and women, young and old, violated law and
custom, sitting where they pleased in buses, trains, stations, restaurants, and moviehouses, waiting to be
dragged off by drivers, conductors, managers, owners,
and police officers. "Every colored person seems to be
conscious of a stepping up of bad feeling between white
and colored," a Charleston public school teacher observed in 1943. "Many of us walk long distances every
day rather than get on a bus since we've had all that trouble."[57] And so it went, more than a decade before Rosa
Parks refused to give up her seat on that Montgomery
bus. (In 1943, Rosa Parks became one of the first women
to join the Montgomery chapter of the NAACP. Two
years later she passed the literacy test and became one of
the few blacks allowed to vote. As an NAACP youth director, Parks helped black teenagers organize protests at
the city's segregated public library.)[58]

Military intelligence and the Department of War documented black unrest and the various ways in which it was manifested, and circulated the information (marked "Confidential") to commanding officers. Thousands of pages, organized under such headings as "Monthly Estimate of Subversive Situation" or "The Racial Situation in the U.S.," detailed black agitation and "subversive" speech, black and white provocations, editorials in the "incendiary" black press, willful defiance of Jim Crow laws, violent and deadly clashes between black and white soldiers and between black soldiers and white civilians. Black undercover agents posing as "city slickers" or "draft dodgers" reported regularly on the meetings they had infiltrated and the utterances they had overheard. The unit intelligence officer in the 931st Field Artillery battalion became so alarmed over the content and extent of this surveillance that he sent some of the confidential material to the columnist of a black newspaper. If the original purpose of this effort had been to identify potential subversives in the military service, this officer believed that it had been seriously exceeded. "I am sending this information to you because it must become public after the war ends. It is clearly evident that the word 'democracy' in so far as it pertains to the Negro is a joke to military authorities." Not until the early 1990s were the bulk of the materials on subversion declassified. By then they had become a valuable tool in evaluating the loyalty of suspect black soldiers. The amount of time and print spent on monitoring "subversive" activity in black America validated the conclusion reached by one army officer in the Morale Division based on the letters and reports reaching his desk, "The threats to the nation were 'first Negroes, second Japs, third Nazis' — in just that order!"[59]

The hypocrisy was too glaring, too conspicuous, too humiliating to ignore.

> Funny thing about white folks
> Wanting to go and fight
> Way over in Europe
> For freedom and light
> When right here in Alabama —
> Lord have mercy on me! —
> They declare I'm a Fifth Columnist
> If I say the word, *Free*.[60]

Forced to accommodate themselves to Jim Crow restrictions and afforded no protection, black GIs in the South found plenty of enemies close at hand. Soldiers who had earlier expressed their patriotism and loyalty were expressing more frustration, impatience, and anger. After eleven years in military service, four of them as a commissioned officer, Clifford Moore managed to survive, even came to love his uniform, but by May 1944 he no longer felt that attachment. "I'm ashamed of it because it represents a nation little better than our enemies."[61] Stationed at Camp Rucker, Alabama, Latrophe F. Jenkins had served overseas for nearly two "punishing" years. But to his consternation and bewilderment, faithful service and sacrifices abroad had produced no changes in white attitudes and racial practices at home. "If this war [abroad] is won by us, (I mean America), then who's going to help us to win ours?"

Living day and night in servitude. In the constant fear of our lives, being less considered than aliens or National enemies, all because . . . our skin's dark. All because we were born American Negroes and not Americans. . . . We are now in Camp Rucker, Alabama; a name that shall live in the lives of the men that live to get out of here, just as much as the memories of Saipan, Tarawa, Pearl Harbor or any of the bloody battle fields of this war.

Jenkins preferred fighting the enemy abroad. "We studied our enemy there, and knew his methods of attack before he came, but here we know NOTHING!" As racial tensions mounted, he felt himself changing, feeling less a part of the war.[62] The same sentiment was expressed by a black soldier in a Southern camp, in a letter to his former high school principal in Atlanta. "I don't know, but I'm positively sure something is happening to me. Whatever it is, I believe it is feeding me with hatred and prejudice, and I eat it, drink it and digest it."[63] Still another black GI, from Tennessee, described his camp as "hell on earth" and questioned what he was doing there. "What I want to know is how in the hell white folks think we are going to fight for the facism [sic] under which we live each moment of our lives? We are taught to kill and we are going to kill. But do you ask WHO?"[64]

Sensing a rebellious mood among blacks, in Birmingham, Alabama, Commissioner of Public Safety Eugene Bull Connor (the same Connor who attained notoriety in the civil rights era) advised President Roosevelt that something had to be done about Negroes who were becoming "impudent, unruly, arrogant, law breaking, violent and insolent." "You have made a fine President," he told Roosevelt. "Don't you think one war in the south is enough? Help us before it is too late."[65] President Roosevelt did not send help. Yet neither did he choose to condemn racial discrimination. By refusing to intervene in Birmingham or in any of the racial outbreaks in 1943, he acted to preserve his party's support among whites in the South.

If blacks were perceived as a threat, the apprehension was by no means confined to the South. Both white and black leaders expressed growing concern about the possibility of a race war. Wartime increases in black income, whether from soldiers' family allowances or industrial wages, enhanced their independence and infuriated employers accustomed to a cheap supply of black labor. Increasing numbers of black men and women opted for better-paying jobs in the North and West, particularly in the war industries, stimulating a major migration from the South. That migration in turn accelerated the competition for scarce housing and recreational facilities, heightened the competition for advancement in jobs, and reinforced the vigilance with which whites policed racial boundaries. The war and the new opportunities it created emboldened blacks by raising their expectations and increasing anger and frustration over the betrayal of those expectations. "What happens to a dream deferred?" Langston Hughes would ask. It explodes, he answered. In 1943 there were 242 racial riots in 47 cities, the worst of them in Los Angeles, Beaumont (Texas), Mobile, Harlem, and Detroit.[66]

Commissions made their reports; FBI director J. Edgar Hoover promised to round up the Communist agitators causing racial unrest; and the Secretary of War blamed the tension on the "deliberate effort" of radical black leaders to use the war for the purpose of obtaining racial equality and interracial marriages.[67] But to an elderly black woman in Detroit, the causes of racial unrest were easily discernible, and she needed no sociologist, no government commission, no J. Edgar Hoover or Henry Stimson to explain what was happening. "There ain't no North any more. Everything now is South."[68] In a poem entitled "Draftee's Prayer," published in 1943, a black soldier gave voice to his fears.

> Dear Lord, today
> I go to war:
> To fight, to die.
> Tell me what for?
> Dear Lord, I'll fight.
> I do not fear
> Germans or Japs;
> My fears are here. America![69]

The very nature of World War II, along with its proclaimed objectives, focused attention on race relations throughout the world. None of this was lost on blacks in the United States. "If we don't take action the Negro will be lost," a black preacher told his congregation. He advised them to "play dumb to the white man" but prepare for what needed to be done.[70] The progress blacks had made during the war in challenging the entire apparatus of Jim Crow only increased their impatience and made the remaining disparities that much more glaring, as bluesman Big Bill Broonzy suggested.

> When I was born in this world, this is what happened to me:
> I was never called a man and now I'm fifty-three.

> When Uncle Sam called me I knew I would be called the real McCoy
> But when I got in the army they called me soldier boy.

> When I got back from overseas, that night we had a ball;
> I met the boss the next day, he told me "Boy get you some overall."

> I wonder when will I be called a man.
> Or do I have to wait 'till I get ninety-three?[71]

Racism acts on the assumed superiority of one race over another. After the occupation of Germany, a war correspondent for *Life* magazine reported that the few Germans with whom he discussed anti-Semitism told him, "Well, we have our Jewish problem and you have your Negro problem. We handled it our way. You handle it almost the same way."[72] But there were differences, as a number of black GIs came to discover. Joseph Jameson found the German death camp he entered "the most hideous sight" he had ever faced. "Some were shot, some were killed with some blunt instrument. Their bodies were a pail [sic] yellow or bluish color. The sight was enough to sicken ones stomach."[73]

During World War II, the German people gave full

rein to an ideology that carried racism to its logical conclusion. When the facts about the death camps became
known, the information was difficult to absorb. At Bu-
chenwald, the task of burying the corpses and sanitizing
the area fell to a battalion of black troops. Leon Bass
found it hard to describe what he had seen upon enter-
ing the camp, not only the skeletal inmates and the bot-
tled results of German medical experiments but the
mounds of children's clothing.

> I saw their sweaters, their caps, their booties. All of
> those things that belong to little children. But I never
> saw a child. . . . If this could happen here, it could hap-
> pen anywhere. It could happen to me. It could happen
> to black folks in America. . . . I often wonder what I
> would have done if, in 1939, my family and I had been
> caught up in this and for all those years nobody, but
> nobody would help us. I would have been a bitter man
> . . . and I thought about how many times my people
> were lynched and mistreated across this country and
> nobody raised a voice. . . . [What I saw] in Buchenwald
> was the face of evil . . . it was racism.[74]

For Paul Parks, a black combat engineer, seeing the
Dachau death camp had a profound impact, emotion-
ally and psychologically. Reflecting on the parallel between the history of his people in America and the fate of
the Jews in Europe, he realized that this could happen
again. "Whenever we acquiesce to the point where we
say it is reasonable to do this to someone, that is wrong.
So when I came back to the States I had one thing in

mind—that I had a legitimate right to fight for my freedom and rights." Paul Parks would later be associated with Martin Luther King Jr. and the Civil Rights Movement, both as an activist and as a public official.[75]

James Baldwin did not visit the death camps in 1945. But he was deeply affected by them, and he pondered their meaning for African Americans. He had been dismayed not only by the fate of the Jews but by humanity's indifference, "concerning which I knew so much already." Like Leon Bass and Paul Parks, he wondered how he would react if the United States chose to murder its black population "systematically instead of by little and little and catch-as-catch-can." Although assured this "could never happen here," he knew that German Jews had been told much the same. "I could not share the white man's vision of himself for the very good reason that white men in America do not behave toward black men the way they behave toward each other."[76]

Near the end of World War II, Richard Wright visited the Schomburg Center for Research in Black History and Culture, in Harlem. The curator had told him about a recently acquired collection of letters written by black servicemen. Wright spent the afternoon in the center's library, reading them. Most of the letters were bitter in tone, complaining of brutal treatment and expressing a cynical view of the war. "The longer I stay in the service," one GI wrote, "I wonder why in hell we criticize Hitler and his Jew-eliminating technique." Another wrote, "I'm not a coward, never was one. I'm not afraid to fight when I find something worth fighting for. But this much I know: If the so called democracies win this war they do not intend to do the right thing [for colored people] any more than Hitler."

Wright left the library "in a daze," deeply moved by what he had read, and he recorded his anger in the daily journal he kept: "Good God, what a sea of despair to swim in! Reading these letters [is] horrible. They are a wail, a cry, but a useless one, for in no single letter was there even a ghost of an idea about how they could get out of their hated lot." "Some world!" a shaken Wright thought. "Why does not the country call off the war with Germany and concentrate single-mindedly on Japan, a nation whom they can hate without reservation for they are colored? I think that the average white man would fight Japan for fun!" The day after his visit to the Schomburg Center, while brooding over the imminent induction of his friend Ralph Ellison into a Jim Crow army, Richard Wright gave full vent to his feelings about the black experience and race relations in America.

> Again I say that each and every Negro, during the last 300 years, possesses from that heritage a greater burden of hate for America than they themselves know. Perhaps it is well that Negroes try to be as unintellectual as possible, for if they ever started really thinking about what happened to them they'd go wild. And perhaps that is the secret of whites who want to believe that Negroes really have no memory; for if they thought that Negroes remembered, they would start out to shoot them all in sheer self-defense.[77]

The war ended dramatically and decisively. "The war is over, victory won," John Davis of the Georgia Sea Island Singers proclaimed in song. "Japs couldn't stand that atomic bomb."[78] For many black GIs, as for many white GIs, there was a sense of immense relief and gratification. If the use of the atomic bomb had any racial implications, they were not evident to those who fought the war. "I didn't have too much thought about it," one black GI recalled. "It didn't make me any difference one way or the other. In fact I was really glad of it because I was supposed to come home from overseas and take a furlough and go to the Pacific. And they dropped the bomb and the war ended before that happened to me."[79] Most black GIs responded in a similar fashion; they found the bombing "necessary and appropriate," a "very happy" occasion (as it made the invasion of Japan unnecessary), and "a good thing to do" at that time (though many later supported the outlawing of atomic warfare), and they praised President Truman's "courage and determination." Some wished that the bomb had been available earlier but wondered if it would have been dropped on Caucasian Europe. Those who had reservations about its use cited the deaths of Japanese civilians ("wished it was their army" instead) and hoped it would never be used again.[80] In an editorial, the *Crisis* thought to ask, "Why did we use the atomic bomb, a weapon so terrible that we, ourselves, feared that its use might obliterate us and all civilization as we know it?"[81]

The persistence, even the heightening, of racial tensions and violence suggests that World War II failed to alter dominant white attitudes and practices. The wartime democratic rhetoric did not reflect realities at home, as this veteran of the Italian campaign suggested on his return home after three years in the service.

> We can never again fit into the submissive position of living as citizens on paper only whereas in actual life conditions are organized against us. . . . We were told that we were going away to fight for Christianity, for human decency and the fundamental rights of mankind. Did we really fight for that Sir? I am an Infantryman, I know what fighting is, it is, in simple words, organized mayhem. . . .
>
> Now we are coming home, Sir. What are we coming to? We feel ashamed and hurt when we look around us and see everybody that comes to the South treated with all the courtesy of American Citizens, . . . anybody, yes, anybody as long as they are not Colored.[82]

Yet in many significant and far-reaching ways—by dramatizing the disparity between American democratic rhetoric and racial practices, by heightening, even revolutionizing black consciousness and black expectations, by motivating blacks to take charge of their own lives and destinies—World War II was a critical episode in the African American odyssey, the first shot in what came to be called the Civil Rights Revolution. "If the Negro can't get what he wants through this war," an activist told a black gathering in late 1944, "he will get it when the boys come home. The Negro will fight for it. We might as well prepare for it because it is going to happen." In the meantime, without revealing their strategy, blacks needed to exploit white fears of social upheaval. "The Negro must keep his mouth shut. The whites are getting more jittery every day." Perhaps James Baldwin sensed how the war had affected black attitudes: "A certain hope died, a certain respect for white Americans faded. One began to pity them, or to hate them."[83]

Not only did blacks lose respect for whites, but those who had fought lost another quality which had been instilled in them over several centuries—namely, fear of whites. And this would have far-reaching implications as the soldiers returned home. "You said they said wait until the war is over, you damn right," a black soldier wrote. "Wait until it's over over here and [the war] will really be fought down there [the South]. I hear these young fellows talk and I know they mean it. A new person will come back home, embedded with more hate than ever before."[84]

In the novel *Devil in a Blue Dress*, by Walter Mosley, a World War II veteran, Easy Rawlins recalls the five years he spent with white men in Africa, Italy, France, and Germany. "I was used to white people by 1948. . . . I ate with them and slept with them, and I killed enough blue-eyed young men to know that they were just as afraid to die as I was."[85] He would have understood incidents like the one reported in Waynesboro, Georgia: a returning veteran responded to an insult from a white man by knocking him to the pavement. As his friend recalled, "All that anger he had, and fear, frustration he had when he was in the war, World War II, just came out on him. And he hit that guy twice and knocked him cold. And he walked away, he didn't run." When the veteran decided it might be safer to settle elsewhere, he went to Florida, taking with him a small arsenal: a hand grenade, two guns, and a long rifle with a bayonet attached. "He was ready for war, he was still a very angry person you know."[86] Occasions on which blacks stood up to insults were becoming more and more frequent.

With the end of World War II, the conviction grew that the way it used to be was not the way it had to be, and African Americans, many of them veterans, would give voice to that feeling in ways white America could no longer ignore. Nearly a century after the Civil War, on new battlefields—Montgomery, Selma, Birmingham, Jackson, New Orleans, Little Rock, Chicago, Boston, Los Angeles—another struggle would be fought over the meaning of freedom in America. This time it would be fought in the context of the experience of World War II, a new generation of black Americans, a rapidly changing world, and a new climate of political necessity. More than a million black Americans had fought a war to make the world safe for democracy. After the war, even larger numbers developed new strategies and ideologies to make the United States safe for themselves. No longer did they feel the need to contain their anger. No longer did they feel the need to veil their feelings. No longer did they feel the need to wear the mask.

In August Wilson's powerful play *King Hedley II*, the title character, a black veteran of the war, wants everyone to know how he feels. "I want everyone to know that King Hedley is here. And I want everybody to know, just like my daddy, that you can't fuck with me. I want you to get the picture. Each and every one of you! And I want you to hold me to it. When you see me coming, that's who you better see. Now they done had World War I . . . and World War II. . . . The next mother fucker that fucks with me it's gonna be World War III."[87]

The bluesman said much the same when he sang,

I feel my hell a-risin', a-risin' every day;
I feel my hell a-risin', a-risin' every day;
Someday it'll bust this levee and wash the whole wide
   world away.[88]

And poet Langston Hughes did so as well when he penned an epitaph for Jim Crow:

Pearl Harbor put Jim Crow on the run.
That Crow can't fight for Democracy
And be the same old Crow he used to be —
Although right now, even yet today,
He still tries to act in the same old way.
But India and China and Harlem, too,
Have made up their minds Jim Crow is through.[89]

World War II marked the beginning of Jim Crow's end, the moment when the gathering storm of black unrest and impatience became impossible to contain.

3 | Fight the Power

We've been 'buked and we've been scorned
We've been talked about sure's you born
But we'll never turn back
No we'll never turn back
Until we've ALL been freed
And we have equality.

> —"We'll Never Turn Back," song from the Civil Rights
> Movement (1960s)

We got to fight the powers that be.

> —Public Enemy, "Fight the Power" (1989)[1]

ON MARCH 7, 1965—a day known as Bloody Sunday—
state troopers and mounted sheriff's deputies, using tear
gas, bullwhips, and clubs, routed and brutalized some
600 civil rights marchers in Selma, Alabama. Governor
George Wallace had declared the march illegal. Twenty
years later, more than 2,500 people returned to Selma to
retrace the route of the original marchers. Coretta King,
widow of Martin Luther King Jr., led the way, along with
Jesse Jackson—a former King aide who, in the Democratic presidential primaries in the spring of 1984, had
won 19 percent of the vote in Georgia and Alabama and
42 percent in Louisiana. The Reverend Andrew Young
also marched; likewise a former King aide, he was now
the mayor of Atlanta, where twelve of the nineteen mem-

bers of the current city council were black, along with half the police force. Another marcher, John Lewis of the Student Nonviolent Coordinating Committee (SNCC), had been beaten unconscious in Selma in 1965 but eventually became an Atlanta city councilman. "What happened in Selma that day was the high point of the civil rights movement," he recalled. "After Selma, the South and the American political system were never the same again."[2]

The mayor of Selma in 1965 was Joseph T. Smitherman, who had once referred to Martin Luther King Jr. as "Martin Luther Coon." In 1985 he was still mayor—but blacks made up 65 percent of the town's population, blacks sat on all of the city boards, and the deputy police chief was black. On the twentieth anniversary of Bloody Sunday, the mayor presented the keys of the city to Jesse Jackson; Smitherman had recently conceded on the *Oprah Winfrey Show* that in 1965 he had been just as guilty for the violence as Jim Clark, the Dallas County sheriff who had ordered the attack on the marchers. "Our hands are just as dirty as his." On Bloody Sunday, the Pettus Bridge leading out of Selma had been a battlefield and the beaten marchers had fled to Brown Chapel. Twenty years later, the bridge and the refurbished chapel were stops on the city's tour of its historical sites.

On March 20, 1999, eighteen members of Congress from across the nation (including John Lewis) gathered in Selma for yet another commemoration of the 1965 march. Retracing the original route, the delegation walked from Brown Chapel down Martin Luther King

Boulevard, intermittently singing, "God Is on Our Side Today." Ahead of them a delegation of children marched while singing, "No One Is Going To Turn Us Around." City officials proudly called Selma "the most integrated city in America." Whites, however, largely avoided the historic celebration. Perhaps their indifference reflected the ongoing controversy over whether whites or blacks would control the commemoration of Bloody Sunday.[3]

In 1962, Governor George Wallace had proclaimed "segregation forever." Standing at the entrance to the University of Alabama, he had blocked the registration of black students. Twenty years later, black voters helped to reelect him, and one black Alabama leader expressed the hope that the wisdom of George Wallace might somehow extend as far as the White House and President Ronald Reagan.[4] It didn't.

Birmingham, Alabama, once deemed the impenetrable fortress of Jim Crow, became in 1963 a civil rights battlefield. It was here that black protesters had to face police commissioner "Bull" Connor and his police dogs, high-pressure fire hoses, and aggressive police officers. But Birmingham capitulated, and it would soon elect a black mayor. In 1963, Chris McNair and his wife lost their eleven-year-old daughter, Denise, to a bomb that tore through the 16th Street Baptist Church, injured dozens of children attending Sunday school, and killed four girls. The McNairs chose to remain in Birmingham. Twenty years later Chris McNair was elected to the state legislature and his eldest daughter enrolled at the University of Alabama. The cell that Martin Luther King Jr.

had occupied in the Birmingham jail was set aside as a library for prisoners. His "Letter from a Birmingham Jail" was framed and hung on the wall.[5]

In 1961 Freedom Riders challenged segregation in interstate buses and bus stations; they were humiliated, beaten, and arrested. Forty years later, they returned to Jackson, Mississippi, but this time the governor greeted them, after proclaiming a Freedom Riders Day. "We salute the heroic efforts in 1961 of the freedom riders and their role as an inspiration to others to follow on the long, often perilous road to end segregation."[6] He also spoke in Philadelphia, Mississippi, where in 2004 a conference and photo exhibit commemorated the fortieth anniversary of the murders of James Chaney, Andrew Goodman, and Michael Schwerner, three civil rights activists. He vowed that justice would be done, and this time it was done. Since 1989, some twenty-three cases involving civil rights murders had been reopened, resulting in twenty-seven arrests, twenty-one convictions, two acquittals, and one mistrial.[7] In 1999, on the thirty-fifth anniversary of Freedom Summer, the University of Southern Mississippi honored the occasion with an interracial conference. Forty-four years after the Nashville sit-ins of 1961, a movement of nonviolent resistance aimed at desegregating the city's lunch counters, the veteran resisters returned for a weekend of programs to dedicate the Nashville Public Library's Civil Rights Room and a gallery of photographs documenting the sit-ins.[8]

In 1925, at the age of seventeen, Richard Wright fled the racism of his native South and headed for Chicago by way of Memphis. Sixty years later, in 1985, the governor of Mississippi proclaimed Richard Wright Week (November 21–28), and the University of Mississippi and its Afro-American Studies Program sponsored a three-day international symposium on the writer whose works had been translated into more languages than those of any other African American author. (Wright himself had died in self-imposed exile in Paris in 1960, at the age of fifty-two.) The symposium was called, ironically, "Mississippi's Native Son." It took place on the very campus where, only twenty-three years before, 30,000 federal troops had been sent to protect James H. Meredith when he became the first black to enroll at Ole Miss. There were now 547 black students (who made up 6.1 percent of the student body), and eight black faculty members. And in an elaborate ceremony in 1987, the blues artist B. B. King, a native Mississippian, donated his vast record collection to the University of Mississippi Library.[9]

Since its founding, Parchman Prison in Mississippi had been immortalized in work songs, in the blues, and in films such as *Cool Hand Luke*. William Faulkner described it as "destination doom." Historian David Oshinsky entitled his study of the prison, *Worse Than Slavery*. It was the place where in the 1960s white guards initiated civil rights activists into a prison life they would not soon forget. For singing freedom songs, nine leaders of the voter registration drive were confined to the "sweatbox"—a cell that was six feet square and had no light or ventilation. From 1970 to 1995, the number of inmates more than tripled and 70 percent of them were black. But by the year 2008 the majority of guards and many of the administrators were black, and Parchman had become a state-of-the-art facility with a modern hospital, an impressive Spiritual Life Center, a fully equipped gym, and a sizable law library. Horace Carter, a prisoner for fifty years, remembered the beatings and shootings and the raw sewage that ran through the place; yet he missed the old Parchman, "the feeling that work counted for something," that the place had a certain rhythm, "awful bad as it was in most camps, that kept us tired and kept us together and made me feel better inside. . . . I'm not looking to go backwards. I know the troubles at old Parchman better than any man alive. I'm seventy-three years old. But I look around today and see a place that makes me sad."[10]

The history of the 1950s, 1960s, and 1970s is a chronicle of the extraordinary changes that transformed the South, some of them symbolic, some of them substantial. The Civil Rights Movement forced on whites a painful reconsideration of the racial protocol. In the 1960s the *Jackson Clarion-Ledger*, Mississippi's most influential newspaper, preached "massive resistance"; it blamed the racial unrest on Communists and it printed racist jokes, among them the editorial comment that the causes of sickle cell anemia had been traced to the glue on food stamps. Some two decades later, the same newspaper devoted a special issue to the passage of the Voting Rights Act. Concerning its part in the racial turmoil, the editor declared: "We were wrong, wrong, wrong." In the

1980s that same newspaper attacked the Reagan administration for trying to turn back the clock on civil rights and for "encouraging diehard segregationists."[11]

Achieving these triumphs had not been easy. Although World War II revolutionized black expectations and aspirations, the infrastructure of Jim Crow, despite the wartime challenges, remained intact. But a different world emerged after the war. Whether as a result of the far-reaching report and recommendations of President Truman's Civil Rights Committee in 1947, the subsequent desegregation of the armed forces, the integration of major-league baseball, the Supreme Court's *Brown v. Board of Education* decision of 1954, or, some years later, the dispatch by Presidents Eisenhower and Kennedy of federal troops into the South to enforce integration orders, the question of racial justice and civil rights began to command unprecedented attention. The rhetoric of the nation's political leaders—the ways they chose to talk about civil rights—clearly reflected this transition. "Why," asked President Kennedy, "can a Communist eat at a lunch counter at Selma, Alabama, while a black American cannot?"[12]

The restructuring of race relations took on a new urgency, an importance reserved for matters of national security. White supremacy, at least its most blatant and embarrassing manifestations, had become too costly to defend or to sustain. In October 1952, when the Justice Department filed an amicus brief in the case of *Brown v. Board of Education*, it explained the interest of the president and the executive branch in the eventual decision.

Nothing less was at stake than the very credibility of the United States in the international anti-Communist struggle. "It is in the context of the present world struggle between freedom and tyranny that the problem of racial discrimination must be viewed. . . . Racial discrimination furnishes grist for the Communist propaganda mills, and it raises doubts even among friendly nations as to the intensity of our devotion to the democratic faith." The brief also cited a response from Secretary of State Dean Acheson affirming the importance of this case in the conduct of foreign relations. "The undeniable existence of racial discrimination," he declared, "gives unfriendly governments the most effective kind of ammunition for their propaganda warfare, . . . and jeopardizes the effective maintenance of our moral leadership of the free and democratic nations of the world."[13] Perhaps, then, one can begin to understand what black sociologist E. Franklin Frazier meant when, several weeks after the Supreme Court decision, he remarked: "The white man is scared down to his bowels, so it's be-kind-to-Negroes-decade at last." The victory, he added, had come so late and for so many wrong reasons that for many black Americans it bore "the visage of defeat."[14]

The black press and black spokesmen, nevertheless, were quick to capitalize on the way civil rights transcended domestic politics. Atlanta's black newspaper, the *Daily World*, hailed the Supreme Court's *Brown* decision by noting what it meant "in these trying times when democracy itself is struggling to envision a free world."[15] Another leading black newspaper, the *Pitts-*

burgh Courier, underscored this point, declaring that the court's decision would no doubt "stun and silence America's Communist traducers behind the Iron Curtain," and "impress upon millions of colored people in Asia and Africa the fact that idealism and social morality can and do prevail in the United States, regardless of race, creed or color."[16]

The elimination of racial practices maintained by statutes and by unwritten protocols deeply rooted in custom required a long and bitter struggle. The white South remained largely unmoved. Rather than support the decision as necessary in the anti-Communist struggle, much of the white South chose to equate opposition to segregation as part of the communist conspiracy. Billboards depicting Martin Luther King Jr. at a Communist training school played into anti-Communist fears that had motivated an entire generation of whites, and in the South the idea of blacks as Communist dupes revived the old terrors of Reconstruction that still prevailed in school textbooks and on the movie screen. For black Southerners, the experience of having their expectations raised and then betrayed or deferred was all too familiar. The ways in which the white South managed to defy and frustrate the court's decision, making it virtually null and void for at least a decade, only confirmed black suspicions; a decade later, in 1964, only 2 percent of Southern black students were attending desegregated schools.[17] The double standard in law enforcement still prevailed: the Supreme Court had made a unanimous decision and then delayed its enforcement.

President Eisenhower talked about "extremists on both sides," whatever that meant. (To an aide, he confided that the decision "set back progress in the South at least fifteen years.")[18] President Kennedy advocated "moderation," whatever that meant. In the struggle against Communism, President Kennedy, like his predecessors, vowed to "pay any price, bear any burden, meet any hardship, support any friend, oppose any foe." Yet in the struggle for black rights, despite the international implications, no such sweeping commitment was made.[19] Both Eisenhower and Kennedy preferred to equivocate. Neither took any leadership in restructuring race relations. Such leadership would have to be provided by black people themselves. In 1955, Rosa Parks refused to give up her seat to a white man in a Montgomery bus. "Somewhere in the universe," a black activist later recalled, "a gear in the machinery had shifted."[20] The boycott of buses lasted some 381 days. Black men and women walked the streets and sidewalks of Montgomery, avoiding the buses. A young clergyman, Martin Luther King Jr., assumed command of the boycott and conveyed a defiance that was heard and viewed around the world. "I'm not afraid of anybody this morning. Tell Montgomery they can keep shooting and I'm going to stand up to them, tell Montgomery they can keep bombing and I'm going to stand up to them. If I had to die tomorrow morning I would die happy because I've been to the mountaintop and I've seen the promised land and it's going to be here in Montgomery."[21] His voice, his intonation, the cadences, the biblical phraseology—all contributed to the power of his message. The Civil Rights Movement was more than Martin Luther King Jr., but it would be hard to imagine the movement without his presence and eloquence.

Half a century later, the scenes, the images, the sounds remain vivid, not only for the Americans who experienced them or watched them as they unfolded, but for a new generation who viewed the photographs and the television footage and heard the "freedom songs." What they saw and heard still resonated. Thousands had taken to the streets, mostly young people, violating the laws, breaking with the apathy of their elders (or enlisting them in the struggle), disciplined by nonviolence, insisting on upholding the nation's professed values and embracing the promise of a new Reconstruction, more sweeping, more enduring than the Reconstruction of a century earlier.

The mood of defiance swept across the South. In city after city, mostly young blacks challenged the laws and filled the jails, enduring intimidation, harassment, and abuse. Children made their way through gauntlets of cursing, spitting, screaming white parents—for nothing more than the right to attend an integrated public school, as mandated by the highest court in the nation. And there were the beatings in train stations and bus depots and jails; the churches, homes, and schools burned to the ground; the bombings, the clubbings, the murders. Few could forget, as well, the marches, the oratory, the raised expectations, the defiant songs (some of them rooted in old spirituals): "Lift Every Voice and Sing,"

"Isn't Going to Let Nobody Turn Me Around," "We Shall Overcome," "I Woke Up This Morning with My Mind on Freedom." All of this made for powerful theater, and the drama often became critical to the success of the demonstrators, if only by infuriating the opponents.

The Civil Rights Movement capitalized on the gains made earlier, in the 1930s, 1940s, and 1950s. Long before Martin Luther King Jr. and Rosa Parks took center stage, black men and women, acting mostly as individuals but numbering in the thousands, had challenged Jim Crow. What the Civil Rights Movement did was to mobilize the black community in ways that captured the imagination of much of the world; these mostly young men and women were willing to use their bodies to give additional voice and reinforcement to the conviction and commitment brought home by scores of World War II veterans. The way it used to be, they insisted, was not the way it had to be.

The Civil Rights Movement struck down the legal barriers of segregation and disfranchisement in the South, dismantling a racial caste system, unwritten protocols, and deeply rooted social customs that had been evolving, sometimes fitfully, over some four centuries. Within a few years, Congress, as historian C. Vann Woodward said, "put more teeth in the law and more law on the books" regarding civil rights than it had in the ninety years since the end of Reconstruction.[22] The achievements were impressive, with striking gains in educational achievement, in clerical and professional opportunities, in skilled labor, in political representation, and in the entertainment and sports industries. Affirmative action opened positions hitherto reserved for whites, significantly expanding the black middle class. From 1960 to 1980, the number of black registered voters in the South more than tripled.[23]

But there were limits, significant limits, to the nation's commitment to racial justice. Although the Civil Rights Movement left its mark on the South, the changes were slow to develop, often taking on a dramatic importance that was misleading. In much of the rural South, for example, an unwritten code perpetuated what was once enshrined in law and in Jim Crow signs. The signs all but disappeared, but the attitudes that had made those signs necessary were not so easy to change. Whites found it difficult, in some places impossible, to learn new ways, to shake off the old attitudes, to give up their grim determination to recover the past, to find new methods for commanding black lives and black labor. Charles Sherrod came to southwest Georgia in 1961 with SNCC and was later elected to the city council of Albany, Georgia. From that perspective, he looked back over the previous several decades to assess the impact of the movement. "Those people who shot at us and blew up churches and all that twenty years ago," he declared, "they haven't gone anywhere. The attitudes are still there. Their behavior has changed because we have got a little power. They won't do anything they can't get away with."[24]

In much of the South, blacks remained dependent on whites for economic sustenance. Making a commitment to the struggle, abandoning accommodation for confrontation, could prove to be a costly decision. Teachers lost their jobs, families were denied credit, mortgages were foreclosed, and any challenges to white supremacy, whatever form they took, individual or collective, faced a violent response. Power still lay with the dominant whites, and every black family had to weigh carefully any decision to challenge the prevailing racial protocol. In Montgomery, for example, black domestics in the employ of white families faced white recrimination when they chose to boycott the buses that ordinarily took them to work. And working-class families faced even greater hostility when they chose to send their children to newly integrated schools. To aspire to be a free citizen and exercise the same rights as whites could be dangerous. "The name of the game is survival," one black activist explained. "Their whole livelihood depends on the white people, the white system. Civil rights, drinking water from a public fountain, eating in restaurants, going to bathrooms—all that is secondary to survival."[25]

It took little time to understand that despite blacks' political gains and despite the cracks in the walls of segregation, many whites still maintained a deep commitment to white supremacy. Although they were compelled to manifest that commitment with more subtlety, the effects were often very much the same. For black Southerners, and for much of black America, the optimism about redeeming America was frustrated and disappointed. Martin Luther King Jr. acknowledged this changing mood. "The practical cost of change for the nation up to this point has been cheap," he conceded. "The limited reforms have been obtained at bargain rates. There are no expenses, and no taxes are required, for Negroes to share lunch counters, libraries, parks, hotels and other facilities with whites. . . . Even the more significant changes involved in voter registration required neither large monetary nor psychological sacrifice. Spectacular and turbulent events that dramatized the demand created an erroneous impression that a heavy burden was involved."[26]

What the movement left undone threatened to make the changes more symbolic than real. But to advance into areas hitherto virtually untouched by the movement would entail costs and would demand extensive economic changes. This would not be easy. Many Americans, as a matter of high principle, rejected racism; they were repelled by the scenes of violence in the South over integrating a public bus, a toilet, a drinking fountain, or a lunch counter. None of these advances carried the emotional weight of new taxes, the sanctity of the neighborhood school, the racial composition of the neighborhood, or a competitive job that paid decent wages.

For all the political gains, the dismantling of Jim Crow, the mass marches, and the optimistic "We shall overcome" rhetoric, many of the same tensions and anxieties persisted and festered, the same desperate struggle for survival, the familiar sense of expectations betrayed, of promises not kept. Even as the Civil Rights Movement struck down legal barriers, it failed to dismantle economic barriers. Even as it ended the violence of segregation, it failed to diminish the violence of poverty. Even as it transformed the face of Southern politics, it did nothing to reallocate resources, to redistribute wealth and income. Even as blacks were elected to mayorships in more than three hundred cities, whites fled the urban centers, taking with them jobs and a tax base that might have supported improved schools, health facilities, and low-cost housing. When it came to changing black lives, black mayors and their machines all too often resembled those they replaced, much like Amiri Baraka's fictional but easily recognizable black mayor. "And what we got here in this town? Niggers in high places, black faces in high places, but the same rats and roaches, the same slums and garbage, the same police whippin' your heads, the same unemployment and junkies in the hallways muggin' your old lady."[27]

The Supreme Court ended school segregation by law, but it failed to end segregation by income and tradition. And this was no longer a Southern phenomenon: in places like Boston, screaming parents and lawless white mobs repeated scenes acted out earlier in the South. By the 1970s, the white exodus into the suburbs, North and South, had made a mockery of racial integration. Whites, it seemed, preferred to abandon the public schools and the cities rather than share power and community with nonwhites. It was a remarkable scene, as many of the urban white Northern liberals who had mandated or supported integration—from Washington, D.C., to Berkeley, California—placed their own children in private schools, thereby avoiding the integration which many of them had previously endorsed in the South and to which they had paid lip service.

The struggle to achieve an equal education, regardless of race or class, threatened to undermine public education altogether, particularly in urban America. White flight was taking its toll. By the year 2000, more than 70 percent of African American students were attending schools in which they and other nonwhites were in the majority, and more than a third attended schools where the enrollment was 90 to 100 percent African American, Hispanic, and Native American. In many parts of the country, as in the Northeast, more than half of all black students attended such schools. Whites, on average, attended schools where more than 80 percent of students were white. Los Angeles and Chicago, not Birmingham and Montgomery, acquired the reputation of being the two most segregated cities in the United States. Although the South remained more integrated than it had been before 1954, it was moving backward at an accelerating rate. The cover story of *Time* magazine on April 29, 1996, said it all: "Back to Segregation: After four decades of struggle, America has now given up on school integration."[28]

Long before the Supreme Court got around to undermining the *Brown* decision, Martin Luther King Jr.'s nonviolent appeals to the white conscience had begun to exact a psychological toll. It became increasingly difficult to wage the kind of campaign King preached. "It is not possible," declared Malcolm X, "to love a man whose chief purpose in life is to humiliate you, and still be what is considered a normal human being."[29] Growing numbers of blacks kept asking the same question: Why should they have to shed blood and risk their lives to be granted what white Americans enjoyed from birth—equal rights under the law? What did civil rights mean to black men and women living in hovels with no food, no jobs, and no prospect for employment in the near future? "I'm not going to sit at your table and watch you eat, with nothing on my plate, and call myself a diner," Malcolm X exclaimed. "Sitting at the table doesn't make you a diner, unless you eat some of what's on that plate." James Forman of SNCC made a similar point about powerlessness with absolute clarity: "If we can't sit at the table, let's knock the fucking legs off!"[30]

Suddenly, white Americans were listening to black radicals articulating a message that brought none of the comfort, none of the reassurance of Martin Luther King Jr.'s "I Have a Dream" speech. Racism, some concluded, had become so pervasive in the American body that it could be exorcised only by shock treatment. Few supplied that shock more unapologetically, and few articulated the frustration, anger, and bitterness of a radicalized movement more explicitly than Malcolm X. He knew his urban constituents; he knew how to work the streets; and, like the bluesmen, his messages echoed the concerns of his audiences. Even as Martin Luther King Jr. continued to embrace nonviolence and interracial unity, Malcolm X was rapidly becoming the radical conscience of black America. But with time the differences dividing them diminished; each in his own way helped black people overcome fears and self-doubts to confront an unjust social and economic order.

The hardening of white resistance, along with a reassessment of tactics and objectives, radicalized the Civil Rights Movement and brought to prominence the ideologies of Black Nationalism, Black Power, and movements such as the Nation of Islam and the Black Panther Party—groups whose influence was always disproportionate to their actual numbers. And new voices suggested new moods in black America. "We gotta make this our Mississippi," declared Hartman Turnbow of the Mississippi Freedom Democratic Party, "Jes' as water seek the low places, Power seek the weak places."[31] At the same time, Nina Simone punctuated that demand with a defiant "Mississippi Goddamn."

> Oh, this whole country's full of lies,
> Y'all gonna die and die
> I don't trust you anymore,
> You keep on saying "Go slow!" "Go slow!"
> But that's just the trouble
> Do things gradually, "do it slow,"
> And bring more tragedy.[32]

Rather than talk about love and Christianity, this new breed of activists proposed to talk about power. The appeal was less to white America's moral conscience than to white America's fear of social upheaval. When King's followers sang "We Shall Overcome," the new militants responded with "We Shall Overrun."[33] One black activist proclaimed:

Now it is over. The days of singing freedom songs and the days of combating bullets and billy clubs with love. We Shall Overcome sounds old, outdated, and can enter the pantheon of the greats along with the IWW songs and the union songs. And as for Love? That's always been better done in bed than on the picket line and marches. Love is fragile and gentle and seeks a like response. They used to sing "I Love Everybody" as they ducked bricks and bottles. Now they sing: "Too much love, Too much love,/Nothing kills a nigger like/Too much love."[34]

What the Civil Rights Movement needed to confront was the fact that large numbers of black Americans had come to discover that integration, even when enforced, was less relevant to their problems than they had believed. This is the issue John Lewis of SNCC sought to address at the March on Washington in 1963, only to have much of his speech deleted by the Kennedy administration and the civil rights establishment. While King preached to the assembled throng about having a dream, Lewis insisted on drawing attention to the betrayal of that dream. Facing the massive crowd of more than 230,000, the largest mass rally in the history of the city, Lewis chose to note who was not there, the most conspicuous absences. "We march today for jobs and freedom, but we have nothing to be proud of, for hundreds and thousands of our brothers are not here. They have no money for their transportation, for they are receiving starvation wages or no wages at all. While we stand here, there are sharecroppers on the Delta of Mississippi who are out in the fields working for less than three dollars a day for twelve hours of work."[35]

Even before the March on Washington, Martin Luther King Jr. had come to realize that his dream was in trouble. None of the marches or demonstrations, none of the sit-ins or mobilizations altered significantly the deteriorating schools, the hostile police departments, the discriminatory trade unions, or the greed of the slumlords and their political associates. Black politics did not provide jobs for the jobless, adequate housing and health care for the poor, or quality integrated education.

The more that black Americans found themselves excluded from the mainstream, the greater were the possibilities for violent confrontation with the visible symbols of white society. The frustration, inevitably, took to the streets. This time, the violence and destruction being viewed on television sets across the country were no longer in a seemingly remote Selma or the Mississippi Delta or Lowndes County, but often only a matter of blocks or miles away.

In 1963 James Baldwin issued a warning to white America, invoking the words of a black spiritual to articulate black rage: "God gave Noah the rainbow sign / No more water, the fire next time!"[36] The decade that began with choruses of "We Shall Overcome" came to an end with shouts of "Burn, Baby, Burn!" Five days after President Lyndon Johnson signed the voting rights bill into law, the most destructive racial uprising in more than two decades broke out in Watts, the largest black ghetto in Los Angeles. From 1965 to 1968, nearly three hundred racial uprisings and disturbances shattered the peace of urban America. Almost all of them were unorganized, unplanned, unscheduled; indeed, it was precisely the spontaneous quality of the uprisings that shocked so many and revealed the depths of black frustration and despair. President Johnson told blacks: nothing of value can be won through violent means (a proposition he did not apply to Vietnam). The FBI, never known for its analytic powers, called the uprisings "a senseless attack on all constituted authority, without purpose or objective."[37]

But they had both purpose and objective: to dramatize the economic issues which the Civil Rights Movement had avoided or failed to touch, to expose the deprivation, desperation, physical and social isolation of the ghettos and the complicity of white shop owners, businessmen, slumlords, and police in perpetuating those conditions. They struck at the most visible symbols of white society: the police (viewed as an occupying army) and the white businesses. The majority of stores damaged and looted were those felt to be the most exploitative in their business practices: stores that sold liquor, clothing, food, and furniture. Not only were black businesses generally left untouched, but so too were libraries, schools, hospitals, clinics, and some government agencies—that is, the institutions that served the community. In the aftermath of the racial outbreaks, commission after commission made its report, replete with testimony and statistics. But the causes were not difficult to discern: an "explosive mixture" of joblessness, poverty, inferior schooling, rat-infested housing, and police brutality—all of which were seemingly invulnerable to mass marches, direct action, and black politics.[38]

Some half million blacks participated in the urban uprisings. Nearly as many Americans, including disproportionate numbers of blacks, were waging a war of destruction 10,000 miles away—in Vietnam. In the streets of American cities, whites and blacks were fighting over the terrain. In Vietnam, the war pitted a wealthy white country against a poor colored nation. Paradoxically, "the most integrated war in American history," as it came to be called, revealed deep racial and class rifts in American society. The burden of fighting the war was borne by the inner city and rural poor—"a rainbow coalition of blacks, browns, and rednecks." Far fewer blacks, Latinos, and poor whites had the resources, the counseling, or the connections that were available to better-educated and more privileged whites. Those who succeeded in turning antiwar feeling into successful draft deferments swelled the ranks of protest marches, and many of them were insensitive to the moral dilemmas of those who replaced them in the draft call-ups.

The war in Vietnam fragmented the Civil Rights Movement. When black leaders or organizations (like SNCC) took strong antiwar positions, most Americans still supported the war and labeled criticism of it as unpatriotic. Americans loved to hear King preach nonviolence, so long as his words were aimed at black folk. But Martin Luther King Jr., the apostle of nonviolence, who had long spoken out against "the madness of militarism," could not avoid Vietnam, particularly after what he had encountered in his personal life and on the civil rights battlefields. How, he asked, could he protest the violence in Mississippi without confronting "the greatest purveyor of violence in the world today—my own government"?[39] Two days after his antiwar sermon at Riverside Church, the *Washington Post* tried to explain the immense injury King had done to his "natural allies" and to himself. "Many who have listened to him with respect will never again accord him the same confidence."[40]

Of far greater urgency to King was the fact that "the bombs in Vietnam explode at home. They destroy the hopes and possibilities for a decent America."[41] He repeated his concern that the amount of money spent to kill each enemy soldier far exceeded the sum that was spent to assist each American who lived below the poverty line. This statistic brought the war home in critical ways, as did the escalating casualty figures. It soon became apparent that the United States could not fight two wars, and was well on the way to losing both of them.

The paradoxes produced by the Vietnam War haunted black America. The military, now the most integrated institution in American society, afforded blacks rare opportunities to make something of themselves. In Vietnam, at least, "Uncle Sam was an equal-opportunity employer." No one examining the draft or casualty lists coming out of Vietnam raised visible concerns about racial quotas. Nikki Giovanni, a young black poet, articulated her anger in her poetry: "We kill in Vietnam/for them/We kill for UN and NATO and SEATO and US/And everywhere for all the alphabet but BLACK."[42]

Upon returning to America, many black soldiers understood what they still faced. "I had left one war and came back and got into another one," PFC Reginald "Malik" Edwards recalled. He enlisted again, this time in the Black Panther Party in Washington, D.C., and explained why:

I felt the party was the only organization that was fighting the system Most of the Panthers then were veterans. We figured if we had been over in Vietnam fighting for our country, which at that point wasn't serving us properly, it was only proper that we had to go out and fight for our own cause. We had already fought the white man in Vietnam. It was clearly his war. If it wasn't, you wouldn't have seen as many Confederate flags as you saw. And the Confederate flag was an insult to any person that's of color on this planet.[43]

Another veteran, J. T. Watkins, came home and found himself spending most of his time hanging around street corners and "jiving" with friends. "Y'know, if I was back in Vietnam, I'd shoot every white guy I could find. They didn't tell me that I was going to be just another nigger when I got back here."[44]

With the explosions in the inner cities, the war in Vietnam, and the heightened rhetoric and new directions of an increasingly fragmented Civil Rights Movement, the controversy over racial change had become too much to absorb for growing numbers of white Americans. The civil rights revolution, as some had called it, proved, in many respects, to be an unfinished revolution. When the crisis moved, as it did in the late twentieth century, from the South to the nation, from the political arena to the economic arena, blacks confronted not only unrepentant white supremacists but even more formidable barriers, described by one observer as "a myriad of interests, far more baffling and morally abstract, federal bureaucracies, corporate boardrooms, glib and amiable spokesmen," all of whom wielded considerable power over blacks' chances for jobs, a livable income, and a meaningful education. How does one reach into the centers of privilege and power to achieve these goals?[45]

Even before the March on Washington, Martin Luther King Jr. sensed that his dream was in trouble, that segregation was only part of an elaborate network of racial inequality in housing, jobs, income, and education. His experience in Chicago had taught him that much. But the tactics of confrontation, nonviolence, marches, and mass rallies that had achieved so much in previous decades no longer succeeded in bringing these issues to national attention. By the 1980s and 1990s, the barriers to racial justice had become more subtle, far more intractable. The problem of how to effect much-needed changes in the very infrastructure of the nation proved baffling. There were no Birminghams or Selmas, no redneck sheriffs or demagogic governors, no police dogs or fire hoses on which civil rights activists might focus their attention, none of those symbolic targets that helped to infuse demonstrations with the theatrical qualities useful for mobilizing the media and public support.

On the contrary, many white Americans had become convinced that, in general, blacks had made it. Civil rights laws had been passed, Jim Crow had been eliminated, the segregation signs had disappeared (some would soon reappear, but only in historical museums). Black men and women had been elected to public office. Many whites thought that opportunities were available for blacks if they only seized the initiative—that a level playing field had been achieved. If the failures of blacks persisted, the fault had to lie with the victim, not in deeply rooted economic and social inequality, not in their exclusion from the economic life of the country. The failure of blacks to succeed had to reflect inferior intelligence, the unfitness, incapacity, and moral, even genetic and cultural shortcomings of the race; it had to lie in their refusal to put their own house in order, to lessen their dependency on government programs and handouts. With politicians in the Reagan era embracing the ideology of less government, blaming the victim had obvious appeal. "If it's their fault, then *we* don't have to do anything."[46]

The same argument had been made a century earlier. After emancipation, the United States refused to face up to the legacy of slavery, rejecting any suggestion that it be held accountable for centuries of unpaid forced labor. The vast majority of white Americans could not be persuaded to accept the idea that if the former slaves were to be given a chance to succeed, they would have to be accorded continuing assistance and protection. Active intervention by the federal government might be required to combat an inequality deeply rooted in history. But most Americans and the dominant political parties rejected such assistance; instead, they embraced the popular notion that the racial problem be left to the Protestant work ethic and the free market, that any preferential treatment for black people violated American values. The Supreme Court validated this judgment when in 1883 it ruled unconstitutional the Civil Rights Act of 1875, which had outlawed discrimination in public accommodations. The Negro was no longer to be "the special favorite of the laws," the court explained; that is, the Negro's rights as a citizen were now to be protected "in the ordinary modes by which other men's rights are protected."[47] Presumably, the Thirteenth, Fourteenth, and Fifteenth Amendments had leveled the playing field and made any further intervention unnecessary.

The same argument would be revived in the 1890s, as if to justify Northern indifference to the savage repression underway in the South. In *Plessy v. Ferguson* (1896), the Supreme Court firmly rejected the idea that "the enforced separation of the two races stamps the colored race with a badge of inferiority." Justice Henry B. Brown observed, "If this be so, it is not by reason of anything found in the act, but solely because the colored race chooses to put that construction upon it." In any event, legislation could not "eradicate racial instincts."[48] The same argument, dressed in a more sophisticated methodology and vocabulary, would find resonance a century later, in the 1990s, in the literature and rhetoric of the white racial backlash. This time it would be articulated by social scientists armed with charts, tables, and graphs that gave new life to old pieties about how to achieve success. Some of the authors shamelessly reminded readers of how they had once marched for civil rights with Martin Luther King Jr. This moved one observer to ask if there was an opponent of affirmative action over the age of forty who didn't claim to have personally offered Rosa Parks his seat on that Montgomery bus.[49]

The idea that the fault must lie with the victim proved comforting to whites, and it was hardly a new experience for blacks. Since Reconstruction, black Southerners had been warned about agitating for civil rights in a society bent on maintaining the racial status quo. In responding to the deaths of civil rights workers, even to the bomb planted in the Birmingham church that took the lives of four black girls, whites had often insisted that blacks had brought this grief upon themselves. A white housewife in a Birmingham supermarket told a reporter that the death of the four girls was "terrible" but "that's what they get for trying to force their way where they're not wanted."[50]

The civil rights arena had been altered. The most troubled voices now being heard, or so it seemed, were those of people who in the past had tolerated or supported civil rights, so long as the agitation was confined to a renegade South and to integrating buses, toilets, and lunch counters. But when it came down to discrimination in housing, jobs, and schools, North and South, when it came down to schools in which children were segregated not by law but by income and residence, when it came down to breaking up "neighborhood schools" and sending their children to public schools with substantial numbers of minority children, and bus-ing schoolchildren across segregated residential patterns—those were different matters altogether, involving difficult choices white Americans were not prepared to make. When the talk came down to housing, to racially mixed neighborhoods, to laws that would bar discrimination in renting and selling homes—this, too, was a most sensitive area, North and South. When George H. W. Bush was a congressman from Houston, no issue brought him more hate mail than his vote for an open-housing bill (he was the only Republican to break party ranks). "I voted for the bill," he wrote a friend, "and the roof is falling in—boy does the hatred surface. I have had more mail on this subject than on Vietnam and taxes and sex all put together." Some of the letters contained death threats.[51]

And finally, when the talk came down to compensatory justice for the victims of racism, when the talk came down to reparations for centuries of unpaid labor, to affirmative action as compensation for three centuries of negative action—those were different matters, too, and many who had once sympathized with or learned to tolerate the Civil Rights Movement defected, particularly when affirmative action threatened inherited privileges and preferences long associated with whiteness. The defections were particularly evident in the North, among the "morally stylish."

By the early twenty-first century, the controversy over school integration seemed all but over, dooming a large percentage of African American students to racial isolation—a separate and inferior education. In 2007, the Supreme Court set back integration more than half a century, denying two major public-school districts, Seattle and Louisville, the right to choose race-sensitive methods to ensure a modicum of integration. The Roberts court shamelessly appropriated the language and spirit of the Civil Rights Movement—"color blindness" and "a level playing field"—to reject efforts to limit the historical privilege of whites and create racially diverse schools.[52] The message imparted by the court could not have been clearer, and it aroused little or no dissent in white America: after all, racial isolation is not the same as exclusion. For much of the history of this nation, debates about the content and objectives of public education had been based on the idea that public schools played a vital role in a democratic society. But in the twenty-first century, with the continuing white abandonment of public schools, they threaten to be undermined by a system based largely on class and race.

For more than two centuries, historian Nathan Huggins argued, freedom in America meant not being a slave, and according to one way of looking at it, freedom meant not being black. "For African-Americans," Huggins wrote, "as for all Americans, the condition of freedom depended on the existence of slavery. With slavery abolished, what could freedom mean for everybody since 'black' and 'unfreedom' were nearly synonymous?"[53] No wonder that in 1865, when a group of slaves in Tennessee were told by a visitor that all slaves were now free, they asked, "Free how?" And he replied, "Free to work and live for demselves."[54]

How free is free? This question persists. Enslaved labor was abolished more than a century ago, but only after 250 years of uncompensated labor. Jim Crow blocked black access to economic and political power for another century. But even with the dismantling of segregation some four decades ago, the images will not go away. Though expressed with more subtlety today, racism remains pervasive; its terrors and tensions are still with us, and it knows no regional boundaries.

Individual examples of conspicuous black success, often depicted in the popular media or in the political arena, mask a larger reality. Even as the black middle class expanded significantly, even as military service offered more career opportunities, a larger number of black Americans were left to endure lives of quiet despair and hopelessness, trapped in a mire of failing schools, bad housing, inadequate health care, hostile policing, and discrimination. The United States remains, four decades after the Kerner Commission report (1968), in critical ways—in how much income most black men and women can enjoy, in what jobs are available to them, in the quality of the schools they can attend, in the level of medical care they can expect, in the neighborhoods where they can obtain affordable housing, and in the futures to which they can aspire—two countries, separate and unequal, including "a large population of interior exiles."[55] The condition of most blacks makes a mockery of the notion of a level playing field.

No matter how the inequalities are measured—by the number of children attending schools in racial isolation;

the number of blacks unemployed (more than double that of whites); the number of blacks living in poverty (double the national rate, including 40 percent of black children); the number of blacks confined to minimum-wage service jobs; or the racial disparities between whites and blacks in housing, health care, infant mortality, life expectancy, and income (the typical white family enjoys a net worth more than seven times that of its black counterparts)—it all adds up to a grim chronicle that reveals a people on the periphery.[56]

If progress is measured by black business enterprise, the number of black business executives is impressive. But there are also far more black prisoners; the nation has chosen to confront the problems of poverty and race by expanding its prison industry. A "culture of control" emerged in the 1970s to handle the growing problem of racially imbalanced imprisonment, compounded by racially biased policing and judging. By 2007, blacks accounted for nearly 50 percent of the nation's prisoners, and 42 percent of prisoners under sentence of death. Blacks were being incarcerated at a extraordinary rate: eight times that of whites. Some 12 percent of African American males between the ages of twenty and thirty-four were behind bars—the highest figure ever recorded by the Department of Justice; in contrast, only 1.6 percent of white men of comparable ages were in prison. Today, some 28 percent of black men can expect to be sent to jail in their lifetime. A black male resident of California is more likely to go to a state prison than a state college.[57]

In 1968, when Martin Luther King Jr. found himself in Memphis to support a strike of sanitation workers, he had already come to appreciate that even the surface changes made by the Civil Rights Movement were in jeopardy. He had come to realize, too, how the violence of poverty brutalized black families and neighborhoods, North and South. His "dream," by his own admission, had turned into a "nightmare." "Why," he asked, "are there forty million poor people in a nation overflowing with such unbelievable affluence?" To open up the American Dream to everyone, to eliminate massive injustices, King now recognized, would require far more substantial structural changes than most Americans were willing to concede—nothing less than massive federal intervention to revitalize America's inner cities, "a radical redistribution of economic and political power," a thorough restructuring of "the architecture of American society." What King envisioned was a fundamental shift in America's thinking, a recognition that the position of African Americans in the economic life of the nation was inseparable from the inequities of capitalism. "Call it democracy, or call it democratic socialism," King declared, "but there must be a better distribution of wealth within this country for all God's children." In that spirit, King announced plans for a poor people's march on Washington, D.C., designed to cause "major, massive dislocations," a nonviolent, revolutionary army of black and white poor demanding the opportunity to improve their lives, challenging the nation's economic infrastructure.[58]

No wonder J. Edgar Hoover pursued King so relentlessly, seeking to demoralize and devastate him psychologically, to discredit him among his own people. With the approval of President Johnson and Attorney General Robert Kennedy, Hoover mounted a vendetta that included unrelenting harassment, surveillance, bugging, and blackmail. To Hoover, King was the quintessential "uppity nigger." Most of all, Hoover deemed him a dangerous subversive who threatened the very social fabric of American society. Perhaps this time Hoover was right. He saw King for what he was: a revolutionary. He would hardly recognize the King honored each year on the anniversary of his birthday, when political leaders are very selective in how they define him. The subversive, revolutionary, radically outspoken King is conspicuously absent, even as his reassuring "I Have a Dream" speech is played again and again—"a sixty-second sound bite." He can be made to seem respectable and unthreatening, even comforting. In these anniversary celebrations, Julian Bond observed, "We do not honor the critic of capitalism, or the pacifist who declared all wars evil, or the man of God who argued that a nation that chose guns over butter would starve its people and kill itself. . . . We honor an antiseptic hero."[59]

Shortly before his death, Martin Luther King Jr. confided to a reporter: "For years, I labored with the idea of reforming the existing institutions in the South, a little change here, a little change there. Now I feel quite differently. I think you've got to have a reconstruction of the entire society, a revolution of values."[60] Even as the campaign to discredit him persisted, King came to Memphis to support a strike of black garbage collectors. By this time, he had come to believe that America was a lot sicker than he'd realized when he began his work. Within a few days, he would be murdered by a sniper.

King had always scoffed at the notion that civil rights legislation alone had created a level playing field. He asked Americans to think of it as a track meet. If a man is entered at the starting line in a race three hundred years after another man, King noted, he would have to perform some impossible feat to catch up with his fellow runner.[61] Expressing this differently, a black youth maintained that equality "is like Whitey holds you by the belt at the starting line until everyone else is halfway round the track, then gives you a big slap on the rump and says, 'Go, baby, you're equal.' Takes an unusual man to win a race like that. It's easier to shoot the starter."[62] Although blacks did not succeed in killing the starter, they did give notice that they were no longer bound by the old rules, by the old strategies, by the old lyrics.

Thirty years ago, black aspirations found soulful expression not only in the Civil Rights Movement and in the oratory of Martin Luther King Jr. and Malcolm X, but in the names black musical artists gave to their groups and songs, suggesting a faith in progress, the belief that America held special promise: the Supremes, the Miracles, the Marvelettes, the Invincibles. The Impressions sang with such certainty, "We're a Winner" and "Keep on pushing,/I've got to keep on pushing,/I can't stop now."[63] Marvin Gaye set the mood for an entire decade in "What's Going On," suggesting alternatives to war and violence: "There's far too many of you dying/You know we've got to find a way/To bring some lovin' here to-day."[64] James Brown boasted in song "Say It Loud—I'm Black and I'm Proud," and Sam Cooke projected the ultimate optimism: "I *Know* That a Change Is Gonna Come."[65] It was the same optimism that permitted Martin Luther King Jr. to deliver his last sermon, in which he transcended his own doubts and premonitions of death to assure his people that some day they would prevail. "I may not get there with you. But I want you to know tonight, that we, as a people, will get to the Promised Land."[66]

But by the end of the 1960s the hope and optimism that had once sustained King and the movement would need to survive incessant challenges and grievous losses. King and Malcolm X were murdered. Curtis Mayfield and the Impressions, who had once encouraged civil rights activists to "Keep on Pushing," warned of the "Pusherman."[67] And Gil Scott-Heron, on the same album on which he sang the unrelenting song, "The Revolution Will Not Be Televised," talked about the post–March on Washington era: "We are tired of praying and marching and thinking and learning/Brothers want to start cutting, shooting and stealing and burning." Born in Tennessee, Scott-Heron was educated in New York and introduced to the work of Langston Hughes and Le-Roi Jones, and his debut album in 1970 had already resonated with Jones's anger.

> In 1600 I was a Darkie
> And until 1865 a Slave
> In 1900 I was a Nigger

Or at least that was my name
And then brother Malcolm came along
And then some nigger shot Malcolm down
But the bitter truth lives on.

Well now I am a Black Man
And although I still go second class
Whereas once I wanted the white man's love
Now he can kiss my ass.[68]

Some two decades after the Montgomery boycott, the songs, the beat, the lyrics captured a different mood. So did the names of the performers: Snoop Doggy Dog, N.W.A. (Niggaz With Attitude), Outkast, Public Enemy, Naughty by Nature, X-Clan, Wu-Tang Clan, Ice Cube, Ice-T, Black Star, Body Count, Blackalicious, Tupac Shakur, Dr. Dre, Urban Underground, the Roots, Notorious B.I.G., Dead Prez, Lady of Rage, Nas, Jay Z, ODB (Old Dirty Bastard). To create their music, they drew from a variety of musical forms—gospel, jazz, blues, rhythm 'n' blues, soul, funk—but they found new ways to use, manipulate, and imagine sound. To compose their lyrics, they drew from the mean streets of urban America, the most ravaged urban neighborhoods of the 1970s, from the black ghettos of Brooklyn and the South Bronx to Atlanta, New Orleans, and Houston and out to the West Coast. Grandmaster Flash and the Furious Five, among the founding DJs of hip-hop, first surfaced in New York (South Bronx). Their classic song "The Message" resonated with an explosive, terrifying mix of desperation and anger, describing the social and economic battleground they called home.

It's like a jungle sometimes, it makes me wonder
how I keep from going under.
It's like a jungle sometimes, it makes me wonder
How I keep from going under.

Broken glass everywhere
People pissin' on the stairs, you know they just don't
    care
I can't take the smell, can't take the noise
Got no money to move out, I guess I got no choice
Rats in the front room, roaches in the back
Junkies in the alley with a baseball bat
I tried to get away but I couldn't get far
'Cuz a man with a tow truck repossessed my car.

Don't don't push me, cuz I'm close to the edge
I'm trying not to lose my head.
Uh huh ha ha ha
It's like a jungle sometimes
It makes me wonder how I keep from goin' under.[69]

Perhaps with Sam Cooke in mind, WC and the
MAAD Circle rapped, "Yeah, it's 1997 y'all and ain't a
damn thing changed."[70] Boots Riley of Coup, an avowed
revolutionary, was arrested seven times for inciting a
riot—a charge he found outrageous. "I don't mind inciting a rebellion, but a riot makes it sound like I don't give
a shit."[71] Outkast, with its "stack of questions" and "no
answers," helped to bring hip-hop to the South. Declaring themselves "Rebels without a Pause," Public Enemy
underscored the obvious: "We're all public enemies, the
black man is the public enemy. . . . We *still* face a dou-
ble-standard every minute of our lives." On albums such

as *It Takes a Nation of Millions to Hold Us Back* and *Fear of a Black Planet*, Public Enemy warned young blacks of media misinformation ("Don't, Don't, Don't, Believe the Hype") and, adopting a song written fourteen years earlier by the Isley Brothers, urged them to "Fight the Power."

> We got to fight the powers that be
> Elvis was a hero to most
> But he never meant shit to me, you see
> Straight out racist that sucker was simple and plain
> Motherfuck him and John Wayne
> 'Cause I'm black and I'm proud
> I'm ready and hyped plus I'm amped
> Most of my heroes don't appear on no stamps
> Sample a look back, you look and find
> Nothing but rednecks for 400 years if you check.[72]

Disenchanted with the Civil Rights Movement, the new rebels embraced their own perspective on the past. When rappers invoked American history, they might recite a litany of horrors seldom mentioned in schools and churches: abduction (the slave trade), theft (their labor and culture), brainwashing (their education), education ("enforced illiteracy," as W. E. B. Du Bois had called it), and genocide (murder, lynching, drugs, and AIDS). Equating politics and betrayal, voting and disfranchisement, they could not envisage a political resolution of the problems black people faced. "The black vote mean nothin," Nas insisted, "who you gonna elect/Satan or Satan? In the hood nothin is changin,/We aint got no

choices."[73] Talib Kweli sounded the same disenchant-
ment with politics. "Back in the '60s, there was a big
push for black senators and politicians, and now we have
more than we ever had before, but our communities are
so much worse. A lot of people died for us to vote, I'm
aware of that history, but these politicians are not in
touch with people at all. Politics is not the truth to me,
it's an illusion."[74]

Hip-hop (the way a person walked, talked, looked, and
communicated) and its distinctive language (rap) raised
the stakes, providing a voice for the voiceless—testifying,
shouting, boasting, roasting. Documenting and chroni-
cling frustration, rage, and betrayal in the inner cities,
the lyrics and tempo dismayed much of the public. It
frightened and outraged people (including patrons of
black bourgeois culture) because of its unruly, anarchic,
even apocalyptic qualities; it defied categorization; it was
abrasive and confrontational. "My life is violent," rapped
Ice-T, "but violent is life/Peace is a dream, reality is a
knife."[75]

Police practices that target blacks have commanded
particular attention, since they are deeply rooted in the
historical experience of black people, North and South.
Excessive force and intimidation have long been used to
remind blacks at every opportunity of their vulnerability
and helplessness. With their brutal, unexpurgated com-
muniqués from the trenches of the inner cities, N.W.A.
entered the Top-20 charts in 1988 with their album
Straight Out of Compton, which included a song entitled "Fuck tha Police" and its classic line, "Some police

think/They have the authority to kill a minority. . . . The police don't want peace/they want a nigger deceased."[76] Ice-T and his band Body Count had a comparable shocker, "Cop Killer," in which a police officer is gunned down as an act of revenge against trigger-happy cops. Houston's Geto Boys added, "Police brutality is now a formality/They're kicking our ass and we're paying their salary."[77] Addressing the persistent question of institutional power, KRS-One asked: Who will police the police?

> You were put here to protect us, but who protects us
>   from you?
> Every time you say, "That's illegal," doesn't mean
>   that's true.
> You were put here to protect us, but who protects us
>   from you?
> It seems that when you walk the ghetto
> You walk with your own point of view.
> Looking through my history book, I've watched you as
>   you grew
> Killing blacks, and calling it the law, and worshipping
>   Jesus, too.[78]

Like the bluesmen, rappers have been called street poets, "prophets of rage," whose work is a distillation of black anger and nihilism. For large numbers of mostly young blacks, rap was the way the world was interpreted to them, a black perspective on the news, a medium that Chuck D defined as "the CNN for the black community." For Ice-T, it was more than that: it was nothing less than "the scream from the bottom." But mostly rappers were young men and women who articulated a growing despair at being trapped in deteriorating postindustrial cities. Unapologetic, they found alternative ways—combative rhythms, street bravado, and racial pride—to express the rage they felt over daily reminders of their debased status. Tupac Shakur, whose mother was a Black Panther, described his neighborhood as a jail cell, a world in which he could "barely walk the city streets/Without a cop stopping me, searching me, then asking my identity." Furious and frustrated, no longer able to contain his rage, he found ways to strike back, feeling no remorse for the consequences. "How can I feel guilty after all the things they did to me?/Sweated me, hunted me, trapped in my own community./One day I'm going to bust, blow up on this society/Why did you lie to me? I can't find a trace of equality."[79]

Since its inception, rap, like R&B, the blues, and rock 'n' roll, has been subjected to every imaginable charge: it's been called blasphemous, obscene, subversive—the sound of the social fabric dissolving. Of course, what sets off the most creative rap from the rest is precisely the degree to which it lives up to these charges. It is precisely these qualities that make rap such a vital and indispensable expression, perhaps the most creative force in American music of the past quarter-century, certainly the most disturbing, intimidating, and subversive. Rap, too, often distinguishes itself by the enemies it makes, by the language it employs. But is rap, after all, any more dangerous to society, any more offensive to our moral sensibilities, than the profanities and lies mouthed by political and self-proclaimed moral leaders?

Some thirty years after the Civil Rights Movement, a new generation of black Americans experienced roll-back, backlash, and resentment, a breakdown in the commitment to and enforcement structure of civil rights—a legacy of the Reagan-Bush era. When Ronald Reagan in 1980 chose to launch his campaign for the presidency in Neshoba County, Mississippi, where three civil rights workers had been murdered sixteen years earlier for trying to register black voters, he said nothing of that crime but instead praised states' rights. This set the tone for the revival in high places of white insensitivity to black Americans. (Some called it the Republicans' "Southern Strategy.")[80] Despite the gains of the 1960s, white racism remained alive and well in America—and in the White House. In black America, nostalgia about previous struggles and black unity only magnified a growing despair. In 1997, a young black man articulated his sense of recent history: "We recognize, more than [our elders] know, the incredible job they did [in the 1960s]. But you cannot celebrate for thirty years scoring a touch-down. Not when they're still playing the game."[81] It is this tough reality that still resonates, as racially conscious responses to persistent inequalities fade away in every part of the United States. "The bottom line is still here," insisted Charles Gratton in Birmingham, Alabama, in 1994. "There was a saying that goes, 'The KKK have pulled off his robe and put on a three-piece suit.' What I mean by that, instead of having a robe and a cone on coming out to lynch you, he took that off and threw it away. He's got the three-piece suit on, but he's sitting as president of the bank, loan officer in the bank, so they're lynching you that way now, economically and financially. It's still here."[82]

With his demonic songs and guitar licks, bluesman Robert Johnson roamed the Mississippi Delta, sharing with his audiences in juke joints, in saloons, and on street corners the terrors, tensions, and betrayals he had endured in his short life. Few black men and women in the early twentieth century could maintain a faith in progress, trapped as they were in a web of controls that encouraged neither initiative nor hope. There was no way to assimilate, no way to separate. Even as they struggled to hang on to their self-esteem, the dominant society seemed intent on denying them their very identity, their very humanity. It pursued them relentlessly. It refused to let go.

I got to keep moving, I got to keep moving
   blues falling down like hail
   blues falling down like hail
Uumh, blues falling down like hail
   blues falling down like hail
And the days keeps on 'minding me
   there's a hellhound on my trail,
   hellhound on my trail,
   hellhound on my trail.[83]

On September 11, 2001, those hellhounds forced all Americans, white and black, to recognize what it was like to live with terror and random violence. It is an experience, a history, that black Americans and Native Americans know all too intimately, since they have lived it for four centuries and continue to live with its legacy. The ongoing response to 9/11 in the nation's media exhibited total amnesia about their past—the heritage of a nation founded by slave-owning champions of liberty. Most Americans reveal a continuing blindness to crimes against humanity inflicted on other Americans, crimes condoned by the state and the courts. How else can we explain the repeated assertion by political leaders in the wake of 9/11 that the United States is attacked and hated because it is so free, so exceptional, still that "city upon a hill," that beacon of liberty.

If Americans needed any further reminder of the extraordinary force of race and class, the fragility of the infrastructure, or the unacknowledged inequalities that persist in this nation, Hurricane Katrina provided it. Americans watched a city drown, a city in which 28 percent of the people lived in poverty, 84 percent of them black. Katrina in the early twenty-first century lifted the veil from the divide Americans choose to ignore between the black poor and the rest of the country.

The images from Katrina left little to the imagination; they revealed what one reporter called "the faces at the bottom of America's well—the poor, black and disabled." Those with means, white and black, got out. The burden of the disaster fell disproportionably on the black poor, living in lower-lying neighborhoods, unable to help themselves, unable to escape the disaster. The poor were left to be washed away; they had nowhere to go, no easy access to transportation (35 percent of black house-holds—more than double the percentage for whites—lacked automobiles); they had no money for hotels or gas. Hundreds of black evacuees seeking escape on a bridge across the Mississippi were confronted and forci-bly pushed back into the city.[84] Historian Mark Naison raised an important question: "Is this what the pioneers of the Civil Rights Movement fought to achieve, a soci-ety where many black people are as trapped and isolated by their poverty as they were by legal segregation laws?"[85] What we were watching in New Orleans, some argued, was a playing out of the deepest, most virulent, most per-sistent of all American tragedies: racism.

Katrina was a forceful reminder that after the Civil War, this nation walked away from the human devasta-tion it had sustained and protected, and rejected any suggestion that it be held accountable for centuries of enslaved and unpaid labor, that government action might be required to correct long-standing inequality. The nation walked away and left tens of thousands of people landless, stranded, homeless, penniless, vulnera-ble. One hundred and forty years later, the bottom line is still there.

No wonder the African American experience has given rise to such classic songs as "Trouble in Mind." Through various renditions of the theme—"Ise been worried in mind"—black men and women have ad-dressed this persistent question since emancipation: How free is free? The song in its many variations has encom-passed enslavement, a tortured freedom, a new begin-ning in the North, the Civil Rights Movement, Hurricane Katrina—the triumphs, the retreats, the deferrals. As a slave song, "I'm a-Trouble in de Mind," it sounded like this:

> I am a-trouble in de mind.
> Oh, I am a-trouble in de mind.
> I ask my Lord what shall I do,
> I am a-trouble in de mind.
> I'm a-trouble in de mind,
> What you doubt for?
> I'm a-trouble in de mind.[86]

It reentered folk tradition in the late nineteenth century as country blues, reflecting the restlessness of a new generation, the first to be born in freedom. McKinley Morganfield (whom everybody knew as Muddy Waters) best exemplifies the song in this generational transition, from the rural South to the urban North. He called it "I Be's Troubled."

> If I'm feelin' tomorrow
> Like I feel today
> I'm gonna pack my suitcase
> And make my getaway
> 'Cause I'm troubled
> I'm all worried in mind
> And I never been satisfied
> And I just can't keep from cryin'.[87]

With the Great Migration in the twentieth century, the song moved to the North, along with hundreds of thousands of black Southerners, and it would be revived in a new setting—an urban and industrial setting.

Well, trouble, oh, trouble
Trouble on my worried mind.
When you see me laughin',
I'm laughin' just to keep from cryin'.
Troubled in mind, I'm blue!
But I won't be always:
For the sun goin' shine
In my back door some-day![88]

Some years later, rapper Chuck D. of Public Enemy added his own refrain, when he welcomed blacks to the Terrordome.

I got so much trouble on my mind
(On my mind)
I refuse to lose
Here's your ticket
Hear the drummer get wicked.[89]

It is all very different. It is all very much the same. In the early twenty-first century, it is a different America, and it is a familiar America. When asked in 1985 to assess the legacy of the civil rights era, a black activist responded: "Everything has changed, but nothin' has changed. In the 1960s Bull Connor threw us in jail, sicked dogs on us, turned the water hose on us. Today Birmingham has a black mayor. Last year he picked me up at the airport and gave me a key to the city. But in the shadow of City Hall I saw black people still living in slums. Downtown I met blacks of the expanding middle class. In the shadows of Downtown I observed a growing underclass. Everything has changed, but nothin' has changed."[90]

Notes

1. High Water Everywhere

1. Oliver O. Howard, *Autobiography of Oliver Otis Howard*, 2 vols. (New York, 1907), II, 238–239.

2. David J. Garrow, *Bearing the Cross: Martin Luther King, Jr., and the Southern Christian Leadership Conference* (New York, 1986), 448.

3. Martin Luther King Jr., *Where Do We Go from Here: Chaos or Community?* (New York, 1967), 45.

4. "Extracts from Letters from Mississippi," in *American Freedman* (July 1869), 20; Leon F. Litwack, *Been in the Storm So Long: The Aftermath of Slavery* (New York, 1980), 220.

5. Rayford W. Logan, *The Negro in American Life and Thought: The Nadir, 1877–1901* (New York, 1954); C. Vann Woodward, *The Strange Career of Jim Crow* (New York, 1955); Neil McMillen, *Dark Journey: Black Mississippians in the Age of Jim Crow* (Urbana, Ill., 1989).

6. Ralph Ellison, *Going to the Territory* (New York, 1986), 12.

7. Nathan Huggins, *Black Odyssey: The Afro-American Ordeal in Slavery* (New York, 1977), xii, xiv.

8. Ralph Ellison, *Invisible Man* (New York, 1952), 13–14.

9. David L. Cohn, *Where I Was Born and Raised* (Boston, 1948), 276–277.

10. Litwack, *Been in the Storm So Long*, 20.

11. Interview with Charles Gratton, Birmingham, Alabama, 1994, in *Behind the Veil: Documenting African American Life in the Jim Crow South*, manuscript collection, Center for Documentary Studies, Duke University. Also in William H. Chafe, Raymond Gavins, and Robert Korstad, eds., *Remembering Jim Crow: African Americans Tell about Life in the Segregated South* (New York, 2001), 8.

12. Patricia A. Turner, *Ceramic Uncles and Celluloid Mammies: Black images and Their Influence on Culture* (New York, 1994), xi–xii.

13. Richard Wright, *Black Boy* (New York, 1945), 227.

14. Ibid., 160, 161; Ralph Ellison, *Shadow and Act* (New York, 1964), 56.

15. Paul Oliver, *Blues Fell This Morning: The Meaning of the Blues* (New York, 1960), 23.

16. Interview with Willie Harrell, Memphis, Tennessee, 1995, in *Behind the Veil: Documenting African American Life in the Jim Crow South*, manuscript collection, Center for Documentary Studies, Duke University; also in Chafe, Gavins, and Korstad, *Remembering Jim Crow*, 37–43.

17. *Washington Herald*, October 23, 1913, newspaper clipping in James K. Vardaman file, Mississippi State Archives, Jackson.

18. Sam Gadsden, *An Oral History of Edisto Island: Sam Gadsden Tells the Story*, trans. Nick Lindsay (Goshen, Ind., 1974), 46.

19. James W. Loewen, *Sundown Towns: A Hidden Dimension of American Racism* (New York, 2005). See also Elliot Jaspin, *Buried in the Bitter Waters* (New York, 2007).

20. Albert H. Stone, *Studies in the American Race Problem* (New York, 1908), 224.

21. Paul Lewinson, *Race, Class, and Party: A History of Negro Suffrage and White Politics in the South* (New York, 1932), 84–85.

22. McMillen, *Dark Journey*, 43.

23. Pauli Murray, *Proud Shoes: The Story of an American Family* (New York, 1956), 269–270.

24. S. F. Davis, *Mississippi Negro Lore* (Indianola, Mississippi, 1914). See also McMillen, *Dark Journey*, 201–206.

25. Litwack, *Been in the Storm So Long*, 286.

26. Oliver, *Blues Fell This Morning*, 208.

27. Philip Sterling, ed., *Laughing on the Outside* (New York, 1965), 78. See also Langston Hughes and Arna Bontemps, eds., *The Book of Negro Folklore* (New York, 1965), 504.

28. Edward L. Ayers, *Vengeance and Justice: Crime and Punishment in the Nineteenth-Century American South* (New York, 1984), 231. See also Leon F. Litwack, *Trouble in Mind: Black Southerners in the Age of Jim Crow* (New York, 1998), 253.

29. John Dollard, *Caste and Class in a Southern Town* (New Haven, Conn., 1937), 359.

30. Litwack, *Trouble in Mind*, ch. 6; James Allen et al., *Without Sanctuary: Lynching Photography in America* (Santa Fe, N.M., 2000); W. Fitzhugh Brundage, *Lynching in the New South: Georgia and Virginia, 1880–1930* (Urbana, Ill., 1993); Jacquelyn Dowd Hall, *Revolt against Chivalry: Jessie Daniel Ames and the Women's Campaign against Lynching* (New York, 1979), ch. 5; Philip Dray, *At the Hands of Persons Unknown: The Lynching of Black America* (New York, 2002).

31. Interview with Ann Pointer, Tuskegee, Alabama, 1994, in *Behind the Veil: Documenting African American Life in*

the Jim Crow South, manuscript collection, Center for Documentary Studies, Duke University; also Chafe, Gavins, and Korstad, *Remembering Jim Crow*, 49.

32. Big Bill Broonzy, Memphis Slim, and Sonny Boy Williamson, *Blues in the Mississippi Night* (Rounder CD 82161-1860-2), recorded by Alan Lomax in 1947, originally released by United Artists in 1959 and reissued in 1990 by Rykodisc. The conversation appeared in the CD liner notes and in semifictionalized form in *Common Ground* (Summer 1948), 38–52.

33. Litwack, *Trouble in Mind*, 290; and Allen et al., *Without Sanctuary*, 179–180 and photo 38.

34. Litwack, *Trouble in Mind*, 280–283.

35. *Savannah Tribune*, May 25, 1918; Walter F. White, "The Work of a Mob," *The Crisis*, 16 (September 1918), 221–223.

36. *The Crisis*, 10 (June 1915), 71.

37. Allen et al., *Without Sanctuary*, 173–174, photos 25 and 26, and endpapers.

38. Wright, *Black Boy*, 164.

39. Howard W. Odum and Guy B. Johnson, *The Negro and His Songs* (Chapel Hill, N.C., 1925), 255.

40. C. Vann Woodward, *Origins of the New South, 1877–1913* (Baton Rouge, 1951), 218; Letter to the Editor, *Chicago Defender*, April 28, 1917.

41. Litwack, *Trouble in Mind*, 155–156.

42. Wright, *Black Boy*, 47–48.

43. Ruth E. Hill, ed., *The Black Women Oral History Project*, 10 vols. (Westport, Conn., 1991), VII, 221.

44. Ibid., VIII, 121.

45. Fanny Lou Hamer, *To Praise Our Bridges: An Autobiography of Mrs. Fanny Lou Hamer* (Jackson, Miss., 1967), 6.

46. U.S. Congress, "Testimony Taken by the Joint Select

Committee to Inquire into the Condition of Affairs in the Late Insurrectionary States" (Washington, D.C., 1872), XII (Mississippi, vol. II), 891–892; Hall, *Revolt against Chivalry*, 140.

47. Theodore Rosengarten, *All God's Dangers: The Life of Nate Shaw* (New York, 1974), 544, 192, 193, 264, xvi, 27.

48. Booker T. Washington and W. E. B. Du Bois, *The Negro in the South* (Philadelphia, 1907), 180.

49. Ray Stannard Baker, *Following the Colour Line* (New York, 1908), 19–20. On the Atlanta Race Riot, as it was called, see Litwack, *Trouble in Mind*, 315–319.

50. Emily Bernard, ed., *Remember Me to Harlem: The Letters of Langston Hughes and Carl Van Vechten, 1925–1964* (New York, 2001), 12.

51. Broonzy, Slim, and Williamson, *Blues in the Mississippi Night*.

52. Robert Palmer, *Deep Blues* (New York, 1981), 72–77. See also David Evans, "High Water Everywhere: Blues and Commentary on the 1927 Mississippi River Flood," in Robert Springer, *Nobody Knows Where the Blues Come From: Lyrics and History* (Jackson, Miss., 2006), 3–75. The 1927 Mississippi Flood inspired a large number of songs, most of them composed by bluesmen. Patton's song has various wordings, depending on the artist performing it. As with many blues songs, the lyrics were often altered from one performance to another.

53. "I Can't Stand It," in Samuel B. Chartres, *The Country Blues* (New York, 1959), 113.

54. "Trouble in Mind," on Bertha "Chippie" Hill, *Complete Recorded Works, 1925–1929* (Document Records, DOCD-5330).

55. Roger D. Abrahams, *Positively Black* (Englewood Cliffs, N.J., 1970), ix.

56. Sydney Nathans, "'Gotta Mind to Move, A Mind to

Settle Down': Afro-Americans and the Plantation Frontier,"
in William J. Cooper Jr., Michael F. Holt, and John
McCardell, eds., *A Master's Due: Essays in Honor of David
Herbert Donald* (Baton Rouge, 1985), 215n.

57. Interview with Kelly Jackson (b. 1894), August 19,
1975, Yazoo Scholar-in-Residence Oral History Project,
Yazoo City Public Library, Yazoo City, Miss.; Laurence C.
Jones, *The Bottom Rail: Addresses and Papers on the Negro in
the Lowlands of Mississippi and on Inter-Racial Relations in
the South during Twenty-Five Years* (New York, 1935), 26.
For additional testimony on the unfairness of labor settle-
ments, see *Southern Workman*, 28 (May 1899), 183; William
J. Edwards, *Twenty-Five Years in the Black Belt* (Boston,
1918), xiv–xv; *Southwestern Christian Advocate*, April 16,
1903; Rosengarten, *All God's Dangers*, 286; John W.
Blassingame, ed., *Slave Testimony: Two Centuries of Letters,
Speeches, Interviews, and Autobiographies* (Baton Rouge,
1977), 648; George P. Rawick, ed., *The American Slave: A
Composite Autobiography*, 19 vols. (Westport, Conn.,
1973–1976), Supplement, Series 2, vol. 4: Texas Narratives
(Part 1), 203, 204, and vol. 5: Texas Narratives (Part 4), 1566,
1568, 1612; Interview with E. B. Roberts, December 11,
1979, Yazoo County Scholar-in-Residence Oral History
Project, Yazoo City Public Library, Yazoo City, Miss.; Harry
Oster, *Living Country Blues* (Detroit, Folklore Associates,
1969), 58; Hill, *Black Women: Oral History Project*, V, 10.
Benjamin Mays (b. 1894) polled 118 of his black contempo-
raries in rural South Carolina: 101 (85.6 percent) were
certain, based on their experiences and observations, that
blacks had been cheated badly by their white "bosses." Seven
disagreed. Benjamin E. Mays, *Born to Rebel: An Autobiography* (New York, 1971), 6.

58. Interview with Milton Quigless, Durham, North
Carolina, in *Behind the Veil: Documenting African American*

Life in the Jim Crow South, manuscript collection, Center for Documentary Studies, Duke University.

59. *Chicago Defender,* July 7, 1917.

60. *The Crisis,* 5 (January 1913), 128–129.

61. Edwards, *Twenty-Five Years in the Black Belt,* 123.

62. Physician: McMillen, *Dark Journey,* 305. Banners: Jimmie Lewis Franklin, *Journey toward Hope: A History of Blacks in Oklahoma* (Norman, 1982), 135.

63. Mark Ellis, "W. E. B. Du Bois and the Formation of Black Opinion in World War I: A Commentary on 'The Damnable Dilemma,'" *Journal of American History,* 81 (March 1995), 1585.

64. Frances R. Grant, "Negro Patriotism and Negro Music," *The Outlook,* February 26, 1919, 347.

65. Raymond Gavins, "North Carolina Black Folklore and Song in the Age of Segregation," *North Carolina Historical Review,* 66 (1989), 412–442.

66. Jane Lang Scheiber and Harry N. Scheiber, "The Wilson Administration and the Wartime Mobilization of Black Americans, 1917–1918," *Labor History,* 10 (Summer 1969), 438.

67. Randy Finley, "Black Arkansans and World War I," *Arkansas Historical Quarterly,* 49 (Autumn 1990), 258–259.

68. *The Crisis,* 16 (July 1918), 111.

69. James D. Anderson, *The Education of Blacks in the South, 1860–1935* (Chapel Hill, N.C., 1988), 261.

70. Elliott M. Rudwick and August Meier, "Negro Retaliatory Violence," *New Politics,* 5 (Winter 1966), 44.

71. Finley, "Black Arkansans and World War I," 261.

72. McMillen, *Dark Journey,* 31, 304.

73. Ibid., 306.

74. *The Crisis,* 14 (June 1917), 62.

75. Lawrence W. Levine, *Black Culture and Black Consciousness: Afro-American Folk Thought from Slavery to*

Freedom (New York, 1977), 197. See also John J. Niles, *Singing Soldiers* (New York, 1927).

76. James Weldon Johnson, *Along This Way: The Autobiography of James Weldon Johnson* (New York, 1933), 337.

77. *The Crisis*, 18 (May 1919), 14.

78. Bishop George W. Clinton, First Episcopal District, AME Zion Church, Charlotte, N.C., to Professor Jesse O. Thomas, Field Secretary National Urban League, September 30, 1920, National Urban League Papers, SRO, Box A2, Manuscript Division, Library of Congress.

79. NAACP, "Lynching Record for 1919," four-page supplement to NAACP, *Thirty Years of Lynching in the United States, 1889–1918* (New York, NAACP, April 1919).

80. The account of the "riot" is based on Alfred L. Brophy, *Reconstructing the Dreamland: The Tulsa Riot of 1921—Race, Reparations, and Reconciliation* (New York, 2002); Scott Ellsworth, *Death in a Promised Land: The Tulsa Race Riot of 1921* (Baton Rouge, 1982); James S. Hirsch, *Riot and Remembrance: The Tulsa Race Riot and Its Legacy* (Boston, 2002); John Hope Franklin and John Whittington Franklin, eds., *My Life and an Era: The Autobiography of Buck Colbert Franklin* (Baton Rouge, 1997), 192–218; Brent Staples, "Unearthing a Riot," *New York Times Magazine*, December 19, 1999, 64–69; *New York Times*, May 31, 1996, February 5, 2000, March 16, 2003; *Oakland Tribune*, September 12, 1999; Jonathan Z. Larsen, "Tulsa Burning," *Civilization*, February–March 1997.

Memories of the Tulsa riot were revived nearly eighty years later when a state commission recommended that reparations be paid to Tulsa's black community. The recommendation proved to be politically unpopular, whereupon a legal team, which included Charles Ogletree of Harvard Law School, filed a lawsuit seeking reparations for the survivors and their families, the destroyed businesses, and the burned homes. The city of Tulsa and the State of Oklahoma asked the court to dismiss the case. The hearing took place on February 13, 2004, at the federal courthouse in Tulsa. The attorneys, representing more than 100 survivors and 300 descendants of riot victims (including John Hope Franklin, whose father had been practicing law in Tulsa), argued that their lawsuit seeking damages from the city and state should proceed to trial. The judge ruled against the plaintiffs, citing the statute of limitations.

81. McMillen, *Dark Journey*, 303.

82. Willie Brown, "Future Blues," in *Masters of the Delta Blues: The Friends of Charlie Patto* (Yazoo CD 2002).

83. Interview with Arthur Brodie, Durham, North Carolina, 1993, in *Behind the Veil: Documenting African American Life in the Jim Crow South*, manuscript collection, Center for Documentary Studies, Duke University.

84. J. Saunders Redding, *No Day of Triumph* (New York, 1942), 259.

85. Charles E. Silberman, *Crisis in Black and White* (New York, 1964), 61.

86. Dominic J. Capeci Jr., *The Lynching of Cleo Wright* (Lexington, Ky., 1998).

2. Never Turn Back

1. The officer is quoted in Lawrence D. Reddick, "The Color of War," manuscript, n.d. (circa 1947), Lawrence D. Reddick Collection, Schomburg Center for Research in Black Culture, New York.

2. Richard Wright, "How Jim Crow Feels," *Negro Digest* (January 1947), 44–55.

3. John Morton Blum, *V Was for Victory: Politics and American Culture during World War II* (New York, 1976), 184.

4. Roi Ottley, *New World A-Coming: Inside Black America* (New York, 1943), 307.

5. Horace R. Cayton, "Fighting for White Folks?" *Nation Magazine*, 155 (September 26, 1942), 267.

6. Ibid., 267.

7. Earl Brown, "American Negroes and the War," *Harpers Magazine* (April 1942), 546.

8. Private Charles Williams to Walter White, Secretary of the NAACP, n.d., NAACP Papers, Part 9, Series A, Reel 10, no. 384, NAACP Papers, Library of Congress.

9. *The Crisis*, 49 (January 1942), 7.

10. Harvard Sitkoff, "Racial Militancy and Interracial Violence in the Second World War," *Journal of American History*, 58 (December 1971), 662.

11. On the attempts to censor and suppress black newspapers, see Walter White, *A Man Called White: The Autobiography of Walter White* (New York, 1948), 206–210; and Patrick S. Washburn, *A Question of Sedition: The Federal Government's Investigation of the Black Press during World War II* (New York, 1986).

12. Washburn, *A Question of Sedition*, 102–103.

13. Paul Oliver, *Blues Fell This Morning: The Meaning of the Blues* (New York, 1960), 251.

14. Cayton, "Fighting for White Folks?" 268.

15. Lawrence W. Levine, *Black Culture and Black Consciousness: Afro American Folk Thought from Slavery to Freedom* (New York, 1977), 253.

16. Malcolm X (with the assistance of Alex Haley), *The Autobiography of Malcolm X* (New York, 1965), 108.

17. Jim O'Neal and Amy Van Singel, eds., *The Voice of the Blues: Classic Interviews from Living Blues Magazine* (New York, 2002), 238.

18. John Hope Franklin, *A Mirror to America: The Autobiography of John Hope Franklin* (New York, 2005), 105–106.

19. Scott DeVeaux, *The Birth of Be Bop: A Social and Musical History* (Berkeley, 1997), 246.

20. Dizzy Gillespie (with Al Fraser), *To Be or Not to Bop: Memoirs* (New York, 1979), 120.

21. Willie Dixon (with Don Snowden), *I Am the Blues: The Willie Dixon Story* (London, 1989), 53–55.

22. Quoted in Charles S. Johnson et al., *To Stem This Tide: A Survey of Racial Tensions in the United States* (Boston, 1943), 90.

23. Charles S. Johnson, "A Memorandum on Aspects of Negro Morale," mimeographed report (Department of Social Sciences, Fisk University, n.d.), 52, Schomburg Center for Research in Black Culture, New York; Johnson et al., *To Stem This Tide*, 91–92.

24. Earl Brown and George R. Leighton, *The Negro and the War*, Public Affairs Pamphlets, 71 (New York, 1942), 8.

25. Johnson et al., *To Stem This Tide*, 94.

26. Ibid.

27. Ibid.

28. Ibid., 93.

29. Interview with Tolbert Chism (b. 1923), Arkansas, in *Behind the Veil: Documenting African American Life in the Jim Crow South*, manuscript collection, Center for Documentary Studies, Duke University; also in William H. Chafe, Raymond D. Gavins, and Robert Korstad, eds., *Remembering Jim Crow: African Americans Tell about Life in the Segregated South* (New York, 2001), 75.

30. Johnson et al., *To Stem This Tide*, 92.

31. Interview with Wilson Evans (b. 1924), in *Civil Rights in Mississippi Oral Histories*, University of Southern Mississippi, Hattiesburg; also cited in Neil R. McMillen,

"Fighting for What We Didn't Have: How Mississippi's Black Veterans Remember," in Neil R. McMillen, ed., *Remaking Dixie: The Impact of World War II on the American South* (Jackson, 1997), 104.

32. *This Is Our War: Selected Stories of Six War Correspondents Who Were Sent Overseas by the Afro-American Newspapers—Baltimore, Washington, Philadelphia, Richmond, and Newark* (Baltimore, 1945), 126.

33. Ibid., 126.

34. Oliver, *Blues Fell This Morning*, 256.

35. Interview with Southern black farmer and World War II veteran, October 1973, in Bernice Reagon, "'Uncle Sam Called Me': World War II Reflected in Black Music," *Southern Exposure*, 1 (Winter 1974), 177.

36. Sterling A. Brown, "Out of Their Mouths," *Survey Graphic*, 31 (November 1942), 483; Joe Louis, with Edna and Art Rust Jr., *Joe Louis: My Life* (New York, 1978), 137, 172; Willis P. Armstrong, "A Toast to Joe Louis," in David K. Wiggins and Patrick B. Miller, eds., *The Unlevel Playing Field: A Documentary History of the African American Experience in Sport* (Urbana, Ill., 2003), 174.

37. Arthur Crudup, "Give Me a 32–20," on the album *Cool Disposition*, recorded April 15, 1942, Catfish Records, Guildford, England.

38. See, for example, Johnson et al., *To Stem This Tide*, 65–67, 82–83.

39. George S. Schuyler, "A Long War Will Aid the Negro," *The Crisis*, 50 (November 1943), 329, 344.

40. Blum, *V Was for Victory*, 208–209; Harvard Sitkoff, "Racial Militancy and Interracial Violence in the Second World War," *Journal of American History*, 58 (1971), 667.

41. Josh White, "Uncle Sam Says," in Guido Van Rijn, *Roosevelt's Blues: African-American Blues and Gospel Songs on FDR* (Jackson, Miss., 1997), 148–149.

42. Richard Wright, *Native Son* (New York, 1940), 14–15.

43. Blum, *V Was for Victory*, 184–185.

44. Lou Potter, with William Miles and Nina Rosenblum, *Liberators: Fighting on Two Fronts in World War II* (New York, 1992), 57.

45. Brown, "American Negroes and the War," 547.

46. The NAACP official's observation is in Roy Wilkins, "The Negro Wants Full Equality," in Rayford W. Logan, ed., *What the Negro Wants* (Chapel Hill, N.C., 1944), 130. The description of Jim Crow as it operated on military bases can be found in the black newspapers, in *Crisis* magazine, and in Philip McGuire, ed., *Taps for a Jim Crow Army: Letters from Black Soldiers in World War II* (Santa Barbara, Calif., 1983; rpt. Lexington, Ky., 1993); Truman K. Gibson, *Knocking Down Barriers: My Fight for Black America* (Evanston, Ill., 2005); Richard M. Dalfiume, *Desegregation of the U.S. Armed Forces: Fighting on Two Fronts, 1939–1953* (Columbia, Mo., 1969); Chafe, Gavins, and Korstad, *Remembering Jim Crow*; and Mary Penick Motley, ed., *The Invisible Soldier: The Experience of the Black Soldier, World War II* (Detroit, 1975).

47. Lloyd L. Brown, "Brown v. Salina, Kansas," *New York Times*, February 26, 1973, 31.

48. B. B. King, with David Ritz, *Blues All Around Me: The Autobiography of B. B. King* (New York, 1996), 91–92.

49. W. Lewis Burke and Belinda F. Gergel, eds., *Matthew J. Perry: The Man, His Times, and His Legacy* (Columbia, S.C., 2004), 37, 61; Interview with George Holloway (b. 1915), Memphis and Baltimore, 1990, in *Behind the Veil: Documenting African American Life in the Jim Crow South*, manuscript collection, Center for Documentary Studies, Duke University.

50. Lena Horne and Richard Schickel, *Lena* (New York, 1965), 175–177.

51. Corporal Robert Brown, 24th Infantry Regiment, November 24, 1948, NAACP Papers, Part 18, Series B, Reel 20, no. 400.

52. Sterling A. Brown, "Count Us In," in Logan, *What the Negro Wants*, 318; Herbert Garfinkel, *When Negroes March* (Glencoe, Ill., 1959), 21.

53. Brown, "Count Us In," 315.

54. Johnson et al., *To Stem This Tide*, 71.

55. Ibid., 116.

56. Brown, "Count Us In," 310, 314.

57. Johnson et al., *To Stem This Tide*, 112.

58. Douglas Brinkley, *Rosa Parks* (New York, 2000), 44–61, 71–72.

59. Quoted in Lawrence D. Reddick, "The Color of War," manuscript, n.d. (circa 1947), Lawrence D. Reddick Collection, Schomburg Center for Research in Black Culture, New York. The letter from the unit intelligence officer, Clifford R. Moore, 931st Field Artillery Battalion, Camp Gordon, Georgia, sent to George Schuyler at the *Pittsburgh Courier* and dated February 25, 1944, can also be found in the Reddick Collection. The Military Intelligence records housed in the National Archives are filled with evaluations of black morale, alleged subversive activity in the black community and among black soldiers, and reports of racial clashes, many of them precipitated by black challenges to Jim Crow practices. For having assembled many of the relevant Military Intelligence materials, I am indebted to Ron Ridenhour, who was until his untimely death writing a book on race relations in the military during World War II, with a focus on what happened at Camp Van Buren, Mississippi, in 1943. I am deeply grateful to Mary Howell of New Orleans for permitting me to examine Ridenhour's archives in her possession. In addition, I examined other

relevant and supplemental materials at the National Archives in College Park, Maryland. On the outbreak of racial violence abroad, see Walter White, *A Rising Wind* (New York, 1945); and Graham Smith, *When Jim Crow Met John Bull: Black American Soldiers in World War II Britain* (New York, 1987).

60. Langston Hughes, "Southern Negro Speaks," in Arnold Rampersad, ed., *The Collected Poems of Langston Hughes* (New York, 1994), 238.

61. Clifford R. Moore to George S. Schuyler, May 7, 1944, Reddick Collection, Schomburg Center for Research in Black Culture, New York.

62. Latrophe F. Jenkins quoted in Philip McGuire, *Taps for a Jim Crow Army: Letters from Black Soldiers in World War II* (Santa Barbara, 1983), 198–199.

63. Quoted in John P. Davis, "Poll Tax Generals: Do They Run the U.S. Army?" *Pittsburgh Courier*, April 29, 1944, mimeographed copy in Reddick Collection, Schomburg Center for the Study of Black Culture, New York.

64. Buck Private (pseud.) to George S. Schuyler, n.d., Reddick Collection, Schomburg Center for Research in Black Culture, New York. ("My name will not be signed to this for obvious reasons. But what I have said is true, so help me God.")

65. Blum, *V Was for Victory*, 193–194.

66. Sitkoff, "Racial Militancy and Interracial Violence in the Second World War," 671–676; Blum, *V Was for Victory*, 199–207.

67. Dalfiume, "The Forgotten Years of the Negro Revolution," 106.

68. Alfred M. Lee and Norman D. Humphrey, *Race Riot* (New York, 1943), 141.

69. Ronald Takaki, *Double Victory: A Multicultural History of America in World War II* (Boston, 2000), 25.

70. U.S. Department of War, Memorandum for the Commanding General Army Service Forces, "Racial Situation in the United States, 25 November 1944 to 9 December 1944," December 19, 1944, Ridenhour Archives, New Orleans.

71. William Broonzy, *Big Bill Blues: William Broonzy's Story* (London, 1955), 44.

72. William Walton, testifying before the Committee against Jim Crow in Military Service, Reel 13, no. 541, Papers of A. Philip Randolph (Bethesda, Md.: University Publications of America, 1990), microfilm, quoted in Azza Salama Layton, *International Politics and Civil Rights Policies in the United States, 1941–1960* (New York, 2000), 61.

73. Joseph Jameson to Evelyna Marable, April 25, 1945, Reddick Collection, Schomburg Center for Research in Black Culture, New York.

74. Lou Potter, with William Miles and Nina Rosenblum, *Liberators: Fighting on Two Fronts in World War II* (New York, 1992), 189–190, 207, 219.

75. Ibid., 241–242.

76. James Baldwin, *The Fire Next Time* (New York, 1963), 67.

77. Richard Wright, *Journals, 1945–47*, entries for January 7, January 28, and January 29, 1945, Richard Wright Papers, Beinecke Rare Books and Manuscript Library, Yale University.

78. Reagon, "'Uncle Sam Called Me,'" 174.

79. Ibid., 177.

80. World War II Veterans' Surveys, U.S. War Department, Troop Information and Education Division, Attitude Research Branch, November 1946, Army War College, Carlisle Barracks, Pennsylvania: 92nd Infantry Division

(Folders 1, 2, 4, 7, 8), 93rd Infantry Division (Folders 1, 20), Quartermaster Corps (Folders 20, 22), Armored Tank Battalions (Folder 29), 2nd Cavalry Division (Folder 1).

81. *The Crisis*, 52 (September 1945), 249.

82. Samuel Wilson to the editor of an unnamed Atlanta newspaper, August 25, 1945, in the hope that his concerns will reach Governor Ellis Arnell of Georgia. I am indebted to Andy Moursund for calling this letter to my attention and providing me with a copy. Original letter in his possession.

83. U.S. War Department, Army Service Forces, Office of the Commanding General, Washington, D.C., "Racial Situation in the United States, 25 November 1944 to 9 December 1944," 3, Ridenhour Archives, New Orleans; Baldwin, *The Fire Next Time*, 68.

84. PFC Van G. Stearns, "In France," to "Dear 'Truth-ful,'" in *New Orleans Informer and Sentinel*, November 25, 1944. I found the letter and accompanying article in a memo issued by the U.S. Department of War, Army Service Forces Training Center, Post Intelligence Office, Camp Flauche, New Orleans, November 25, 1944 (Confidential), Riden-hour Archives, New Orleans.

85. Walter Mosley, *Devil in a Blue Dress* (New York, 1990), 9.

86. Interview with Wilhelmina Baldwin, Tuskegee, Alabama, July 19, 1994, in *Behind the Veil: Documenting African American Life in the Jim Crow South*, manuscript collection, Center for Documentary Studies, Duke University.

87. August Wilson, *King Hedley II* (New York, 2005), 58.

88. Levine, *Black Culture and Black Consciousness*, 418.

89. Langston Hughes, *Jim Crow's Last Stand*, Race and Culture series, no. 2, Negro Publication Society of America (Atlanta, 1943), 29.

3. Fight the Power

1. "Fight the Power," by Chuck D., Hank Shocklee, Keith Shocklee, and Eric T. Sadler, © 1990 Songs of Universal, Inc., Reach Global Songs, Terrordome Music Publ. LLC, and Shocklee Music (BMI); used by permission, all rights reserved.

2. William E. Schmidt, "Selma, Twenty Years after the Rights March," *New York Times*, March 1, 1985, A1; William E. Schmidt, "March for Rights Resounds after Twenty Years," *New York Times*, March 8, 1985, A16; Ronald Smothers, "A Selma March Relives Those First Steps of '65," March 5, 1990, B6; Peter Applebome, "In Selma, Everything and Nothing Changed," *New York Times*, August 2, 1994, A1; Peter Applebome, "From Atlanta to Birmingham, Blur of Progress and Stagnation," *New York Times*, August 3, 1994, A14; "Civil Rights Veteran Is Honored in Selma," *New York Times*, March 9, 1998, A15; D. L. Stanley, "Lewis, Other Lawmakers Re-Create Historic Selma March," *Atlanta Inquirer*, March 20, 1999, 1; Amy Bach, "Selma Is Still Selma," *The Nation*, September 18–25, 2000, 6–9.

3. Schmidt, "March for Rights Resounds after Twenty Years," A16; Stanley, "Lewis, Other Lawmakers Re-Create Historic Selma March"; Bach, "Selma Is Still Selma," 6–9.

4. Schmidt, "March for Rights Resounds after Twenty Years," A16.

5. "Progress in 1973: Minority Political Advances," *Oakland Post*, February 13, 1974, 1; Howell Raines, "The Birmingham Bombing," *New York Times*, July 24, 1983, A12.

6. "Mississippi Welcomes Freedom Riders," *New York Times*, November 10, 2001, A11.

7. Gary Younge, "Racism Rebooted: Philadelphia, Mississippi, Then and Now," *The Nation*, July 11, 2005,

11–14. "United States: Justice Delayed—Atoning for Segregation," *The Economist*, June 18, 2005, 46.

8. Nicolaus Mills, "Mississippi Freedom Summer Thirty-Five Years Later," *Dissent* (Summer 1999), 1–3; "One City, Two Peoples," *Nashville Scene*, January 29–February 4, 2004, 1–9.

9. "Mississippi's Native Son: The University of Mississippi Presents an International Symposium on Richard Wright (1908–1960)," sponsored by the Afro-American Studies Program, Oxford, Mississippi, 1985; Edwin McDowell, "Mississippi Honors a 'Native Son' Who Fled," *New York Times*, November 23, 1985.

10. David M. Oshinsky, *Worse Than Slavery: Parchman Farm and the Ordeal of Jim Crow Justice* (New York, 1996), 229–236, 255; Raymond Arsenault, *Freedom Riders: 1961 and the Struggle for Racial Justice* (New York, 2006), 325–327, 349–365; Taylor Branch, *Parting the Waters: America in the King Years, 1954–1963* (New York, 1988), 483–485; James Farmer, *Lay Bare the Heart: An Autobiography of the Civil Rights Movement* (New York, 1985), 22–32.

11. Tom Etheridge, "Courageous Speech," *Jackson Clarion-Ledger*, September 15, 1962, 1; Gene Wirth, "Place Assured in History for Fearless Ross Barnett," *Jackson Clarion-Ledger*, September 15, 1962, 1; David Hampton, "Perspective," *Jackson Clarion-Ledger*, June 19, 2005, 1G; Sid Salter, "A Fresh Take on State's Ghosts," *Jackson Clarion-Ledger*, February 24, 2002, 1G; see also Jack Bass and Tom E. Terrill, *The American South Comes of Age* (New York, 1986), 397; Susan Weill, *In a Madhouse's Din: Civil Rights Coverage by Mississippi's Daily Press, 1948–1968* (Westport, Conn., 2002), 37.

12. Quoted in Thomas J. Friedman, "Cold War without End," *New York Times Magazine*, August 22, 1993, 45; Leon

F. Litwack, "Unfinished Business," *Journal of Blacks in Higher Education* (Spring 2005), 96–98.

13. Brief for the United States as Amicus Curiae at 6 and 7, *Brown*, 347 U.S. 483 (1954). Online at curiae.law.yale.edu/pdf/347-483/022.pdf.

14. Quoted in Harold Isaacs, "Integration and the Negro Mood," *Commentary* (December 1962), 488.

15. *Atlanta Daily World*, May 18, 1954.

16. *Pittsburgh Courier*, May 18, 1954; Waldo E. Martin, *Brown v. Board of Education* (Boston, 1998), 202.

17. Harvard Sitkoff, *The Struggle for Black Equality, 1954–1980* (New York, 1981), 38.

18. Ibid., 25.

19. Ibid., 106.

20. Eldridge Cleaver, *Soul on Ice* (New York, 1968), 194.

21. Martin Luther King Jr., sermon delivered January 27, 1957, at Dexter Avenue Baptist Church, Montgomery, Alabama; *Montgomery Advertiser*, January 28, 1957, A2; *Pittsburgh Courier*, February 9, 1957, 2; David J. Garrow, "Martin Luther King, Jr., and the Spirit of Leadership," *Journal of American History*, 74 (September 1987), 438–447 (issue titled *A Round Table: Martin Luther King, Jr.*).

22. Quote in Charles E. Silberman, "Beware the Day They Change Their Minds," *Fortune Magazine*, 1965 (issued as separate report; month not stated).

23. Schmidt, "Selma, Twenty Years after the Rights March," A1.

24. E. R. Shipp, "Across the Rural South, Segregation as Usual," *New York Times*, April 27, 1985, 1.

25. Ibid.

26. Martin Luther King Jr., *Where Do We Go From Here: Chaos or Community?* (New York, 1967), 5.

27. Amiri Baraka (LeRoi Jones), *Tales of the Out and the Gone* (New York, 2007), 31–32.

28. "The End of Integration," *Time*, April 29, 1996, 39–45; Richard Kluger, *Simple Justice: The History of Brown v. Board of Education and Black America's Struggle for Equality* (New York, 2004), 774–776.

29. Quoted in Juan Williams and Quinton Dixie, *This Far by Faith: Stories from the African American Religious Experience* (New York, 2003), 228.

30. Malcolm X, "The Ballot or the Bullet," *Malcolm X Speaks* (New York, 1965), 26; James Forman, in *Eyes on the Prize* (First Series), Episode 6, "Bridge to Freedom" (Blackside, 1965, videocassette).

31. Quoted in Stokely Carmichael with Ekwueme Michael Thelwell, *Ready for Revolution: The Life and Struggles of Stokely Carmichael (Kwame Ture)* (New York, 2003), 501.

32. Nina Simone, on the album *Four Women* (Philips Recordings, 2003). The song was recorded in 1963.

33. King, *Where Do We Go From Here?* 26.

34. Clayborne Carson, *In Struggle: SNCC and the Black Awakening of the 1960s* (Cambridge, Mass., 1981), 237. See also Julius Lester, *Look Out Whitey!* (New York, 1968), 107.

35. John Lewis, "The March on Washington," *Commemoration*, April 13, 2003, video of speech by John Lewis at the March on Washington, August 28, 1963.

36. James Baldwin, *The Fire Next Time* (New York, 1963), title page.

37. Untitled Report, Federal Bureau of Investigation, U.S. Department of Justice, September 18, 1964, quoted in Harry S. Ashmore, *Civil Rights and Wrongs: A Memoir of Race and Politics, 1944–1996*, rev. ed. (Columbia, S.C., 1997), 191.

38. Taylor Branch, *At Canaan's Edge: America in the King Years, 1965–1968* (New York, 2006), 630–634; Sitkoff, *Struggle for Black Equality*, 200–208.

39. Martin Luther King Jr., "A Time to Break Silence," sermon delivered at a meeting of Clergy and Laity Concerned, Riverside Church, New York City, April 4, 1967, in *A Testament of Hope: The Essential Writings of Martin Luther King, Jr.*, ed. James M. Washington (San Francisco, 1986), 231–244.

40. *Washington Post*, April 6, 1967, A20.

41. Martin Luther King Jr., quoted in U.S. Senate, 89th Congress, 2nd session, Hearings before the Subcommittee on Executive Reorganization of the Committee on Government Operations, The Federal Role in Urban Affairs (Washington, D.C., 1967), 2970; Adam Fairclough, "Martin Luther King, Jr., and the War in Vietnam," *Phylon*, 45 (January–March 1984), 28; Sitkoff, *Struggle for Equality*, 219.

42. Nikki Giovanni, "The True Import of Present Dialogue, Black vs. Negro," in *The Collected Poetry of Nikki Giovanni* (New York, 1996), 19–20.

43. Wallace Terry, *Bloods: An Oral History of the Vietnam War by Black Veterans* (New York, 1984), 13–14.

44. *Newsweek Magazine*, November 20, 1967, 41.

45. Marshall Frady, "Prophet with Honor," *New York Review of Books*, October 27, 1983, 83.

46. David L. Karp, "Following the Color Line," *The Nation*, April 24, 1995, 57.

47. Civil Rights Cases, 109 U.S. 3 (1883), in Henry Steele Commager, ed., *Documents of American History*, 4th ed., 2 vols. (New York, 1948), II, No. 292, 86–88.

48. *Plessy v. Ferguson*, 163 U.S. 537 (1896), in Brook

Thomas, ed., *Plessy v. Ferguson: A Brief History with Documents* (Boston, 1997), 41–60.

49. Katha Pollitt in *The Nation*, May 12, 1997.

50. Robert E. Baker, "Grief and Fear Shared in Birmingham," *Washington Post*, September 19, 1963.

51. Philip A. Klinker, with Rogers M. Smith, *The Unsteady March: The Rise and Decline of Racial Equality in America* (Chicago, 1999), 284–285.

52. Nancy MacLean, "The Scary Origins of Chief Justice Roberts's Decision Opposing the Use of Race to Promote Integration," August 6, 2007, History News Network, George Mason University, hnn.us/articles/41501.html; "Roberts Rules," *New Republic*, July 23, 2007, 1, 4; Patricia J. Williams, "Mourning in America," *The Nation*, July 30–August 6, 2007, 4–5.

53. Nathan Irvin Huggins, *Revelations: American History, American Myths* (New York, 1995), 280.

54. Leon F. Litwack, *Been in the Storm So Long: The Aftermath of Slavery* (New York, 1979), 220.

55. Kerner Commission, *Report of the National Advisory Commission on Civil Disorders* (Washington, D.C., 1968); Frady, "Prophet with Honor," 79.

56. Eric Alterman, "We've Become More Unequal and That Matters," *Altercation* (blog), July 30, 2007, available online from History News Network at hnn.us/roundup/entries/41414.html; "Under George Bush, Blacks Are Giving Back the Economic Gains Achieved during the Clinton Years," *Journal of Blacks in Higher Education* (Summer 2006), 80; Harrison Rainie, with Scott Minerbrook, Matthew Cooper, Constance Johnson, Steven V. Roberts, and Ted Gest, "Black and White in America," *U.S. News and World Report*, July 22, 1991, 18–21; Constance L. Hays, "Study

Says Blacks, More Than Other Groups, Face Segregation, *New York Times*, November 23, 1988; Tom Wicker, "In the Nation: And Still Two Nations," *New York Times*, January 23, 1984, A21.

57. Glenn C. Loury, "Why Are So Many Americans in Prison? Race and the Transformation of Criminal Justice," *Boston Review*, July–August 2007, 7–10; John Edgar Wideman, "Doing Time: Marking Race," *The Nation*, August 27–September 3, 2007, 29–36; Orlando Patterson, "Jena, O.J., and the Jailing of Black America," *New York Times*, September 30, 2007; Jason De Parle, "The American Prison Nightmare," *New York Review of Books*, April 12, 2007, 33–36.

58. Martin Luther King Jr., "Where Do We Go From Here?" last SCLC presidential address, in *A Testament of Hope*, 245–252; Martin Luther King Jr., *Why We Can't Wait* (New York, 1964), 143; David J. Garrow, *Bearing the Cross: Martin Luther King, Jr., and the Southern Christian Leadership Conference* (New York, 1986), 426–427; Thomas F. Jackson, *From Civil Rights to Human Rights: Martin Luther King, Jr., and the Struggle for Economic Justice* (Philadelphia, 2006), 230; Stephen B. Oates, *Let the Trumpet Sound: The Life of Martin Luther King, Jr.* (New York, 1994), 450.

59. Paul M. Gaston, "Missing Martin," *Southern Changes*, 25, nos. 1–4 (2003), 6.

60. Martin Luther King Jr., interview with David Halberstam, "Notes from the Bottom of the Mountain," *Harper's*, June 1968, 40–43; also quoted in Garrow, *Bearing the Cross*, 562.

61. Martin Luther King Jr., testimony before the National Advisory Commission on Civil Disorders, 1967, quoted in

Drew D. Hansen, *The Dream: Martin Luther King, Jr., and the Speech That Inspired a Nation* (New York, 2003), 224.

62. Quoted in Russell Sackett, "Plotting a War on Whitey," *Life*, June 10, 1966.

63. The Impressions, "We're a Winner," words and music by Curtis Mayfield (ABC-Paramount, 1967); "Keep On Pushing," words and music by Curtis Mayfield (Paramount, 1964).

64. Marvin Gaye, "What's Going On," words and music by Al Cleveland, Renaldo Benson, and Marvin Gaye (Tamia, 1971).

65. James Brown, "Say It Loud—I'm Black and I'm Proud," written by James Brown and Alfred Ellis, on the album *Say It Loud—I'm Black and I'm Proud* (King, 1968); Sam Cooke, "A Change Is Gonna Come," on the album *Ain't That Good News* (RCA Victor, 1964).

66. Martin Luther King Jr., "I See the Promised Land," in *Testament of Hope*, 286.

67. The Impressions, "Keep On Pushing," words and music by Curtis Mayfield (Paramount, 1964); Curtis Mayfield, "Pusherman," *Superfly*, film soundtrack (Curtom, 1972).

68. Gil Scott-Heron, "Evolution (and Flashback)," on the album *Evolution (and Flashback): The Very Best of Gil Scott-Heron*, recorded 1970–1972 (RCA Victor, 1999); transcript excerpted in Alan Kaufman and S. A. Griffin, eds., *The Outlaw Bible of American Poetry* (New York, 1999), 287–288.

69. Grandmaster Flash and the Furious Five, "The Message," written by Sugar Hill session musician Ed "Duke Bootee" Fletcher and Furious Five's MC, Melle Mel (Sugar Hill, 1982). Lyrics copyright © EMI Music Publishing, Sony/ATV Music Publishing LLC.

70. WC and the MAAD Circle, "Ain't a Damn Thing Changed" (Priority Records, 1991).

71. David Segal, "The Rapper's Red Glare: Boots Riley Hopes the Coup's Album Will Rattle the Capitalists, and Make Some Change," *Washington Post*, May 22, 2002, C1. I am indebted to Molly Hooper for bringing this article to my attention.

72. Jeff Chang, *Can't Stop Won't Stop: A History of the Hip-Hop Generation* (New York, 2005), 246–261. "Fight the Power," by Chuck D., Hank Shocklee, Keith Shocklee, and Eric T. Sadler, © 1990 Songs of Universal, Inc., Reach Global Songs, Terrordome Music Publ. LLC, and Shocklee Music (BMI); used by permission, all rights reserved.

73. "American Way," by Nas, Garry Shider, David Spradley, George Clinton Jr., Kamaal Fareed, and Kelis, © 2004 Universal Music—Z Tunes LLC, Ill Will Music, Inc., Southfield Music, Inc., Betta Like My Music, EMI/April Music, Inc., and Issy & Nemo Tunes (ASCAP), and Bridgeport Music (BMI); all rights for Ill Will Music, Inc. administered by Universal Music—Z Tunes LLC (ASCAP); used by permission, all rights reserved. Title "American Way" written by Nasir Jones/Kamaal Fareed/Kelis Rogers/George Clinton Jr./Garry M. Shider/David L. Spradley, © copyright 2004 by Bridgeport Music, Inc. (BMI)/Southfield Music, Inc., and copublishers according to their instructions; all rights reserved, used by permission.

74. Jeff Chang, "'Stakes Is High': Conscious Rap, Neosoul and the Hip-Hop Generation," *The Nation*, January 13–20, 2003, 20.

75. Ice-T, "Colors," on the album *Colors*, film soundtrack (Warner Brothers Records, 1990).

76. N.W.A., "Fuck tha Police," on the album *Straight out of Compton* (Priority Records, 1989).

77. Geto Boys, "City under Siege" (Asylum Records, 1990).

78. "Who Protects Us from You?" by KRS-One, © 1989 Universal Music—Z Tunes LLC; used by permission, all rights reserved.

79. "Trapped," Tupac Shakur, Ramon Gooden, Playa Playa, Dank, and Wiz, © 1991 Universal Music Corp. (ASCAP), Universal Music—Z Songs (BMI), Playa Playa designee, Dank designee, Wiz designee; used by permission, all rights reserved.

80. Douglas E. Kneeland, "Reagan Campaigns at Mississippi Fair," *New York Times*, August 4, 1980; "Ham, Grits, and Oratory: Reagan Opens Campaign at a Dixie County Fair," *Los Angeles Times*, August 4, 1980; Lou Cannon, "Reagan Campaigning from County Fair to Urban League," *Washington Post*, August 4, 1980; Andrew Young, "Chilling Words in Neshoba County," *Washington Post*, August 11, 1980; "Shades of the Klan: Reagan's Talk of States' Rights Is Scary," *Los Angeles Times*, August 13, 1980. Controversy over the Reagan campaign was revived in the *New York Times*, November 9, 12, 13, 15, 19, 22, 2007. See also Joseph Crespino, *In Search of Another Country: Mississippi and the Conservative Counterrevolution* (Princeton, N.J., 2007).

81. John Leland and Allison Samuels, "The New Generation Gap," *Newsweek*, March 17, 1997, 57.

82. Interview with Charles Gratton, Birmingham, Alabama, 1994, in *Behind the Veil: Documenting African American Life in the Jim Crow South*, manuscript collection, Center for Documentary Studies, Duke University.

83. Robert Johnson, "Hellhound on My Trail," on the album *Robert Johnson: The Complete Recordings* (Columbia, C2K 46222).

84. "Through the Eye of Katrina: The Past as Prologue?" *Journal of American History*, 94 (December, 2007); David Dante Troutt, ed., *After the Storm: Black Intellectuals Explore the Meaning of Hurricane Katrina* (New York, 2006); Michael Eric Dyson, *Come Hell or High Water: Hurricane Katrina and the Color of Disaster* (New York, 2006); Jonathan Alter, "Poverty, Race and Katrina: Lessons of a National Shame," *Newsweek*, September 19, 2005.

85. Mark Naison, quoted in Jason DeParle, "Broken Levees, Unbroken Barriers," *New York Times*, September 4, 2005, 4; "Mark Naison on Race, Class, and the Disaster," *The Nation* (blog), online at www.thenation.com/blogs/edcut?pid=19934.

86. "I'm a-Trouble in de Mind," in William Francis Alle, Charles Pickard Ware, and Lucy McKim Garrison, comps., *Slave Songs of the United States* (New York, 1867), 30–31.

87. Muddy Waters, "I Be's Troubled," on the album *Muddy Waters: Library of Congress Recordings, 1941–1942, and Early Commercial Recordings, 1946–1950* (Document Records, DOCD-5146). See also Robert Palmer, *Deep Blues* (New York, 1981), 3–7, 12–17.

88. "Trouble in Mind Blues," on the album *Richard M. Jones and the Blues Singers, 1923–1938* (Document Records, DOCD-5390); Henry Louis Gates Jr. and Nellie Y. McKay, eds., *The Norton Anthology of African American Literature* (New York, 1997), 29.

89. "Welcome to the Terrordome," by Chuck D. and Keith Shocklee, © 1990 Songs of Universal, Inc., Reach Global Songs and Bring The Noize, Inc. (BMI); used by permission, all rights reserved.

90. *Christian Science Monitor*, November 29, 1985; Schmidt, "Selma, Twenty Years after the Rights March," A1.

Acknowledgments

In 2004, I was invited to give the Nathan I. Huggins Lectures at the W. E. B. Du Bois Institute for African and African-American Research at Harvard University. I very much appreciated that opportunity, for reasons that may not have been apparent to the audience. For some forty years Nathan and I had known each other, meeting as undergraduates at Berkeley, sharing the same politics, the same commitment to social activism, and a passionate interest in the history we would ultimately teach and research. After Berkeley, that friendship endured, often at long distance. I always admired his insatiable curiosity, his intellectual engagement, and his playful wit and spirit. He asked the toughest questions, and he persisted until he got answers. To the very end, he fought the good fight, never yielding to complacency, indifference, or accommodation. He envisioned a curriculum that would reflect the racial and cultural diversity of this country, and he challenged the Eurocentric bias in education. "How," he asked, "do we get people who believe they are the center of the universe to move over?" That was vintage Huggins, and the question he posed more than a decade ago resonates with as much force and relevance today.

Initially, the audience for these lectures, in their various versions, consisted of my students at Berkeley, the more than 25,000 students I taught there over forty-two years, most of them in the survey U.S. history course and in the upper-division course in the history of African Americans and race relations. I remain grateful to them for their responses, questions, critiques, and encouragement. I owe thanks to the Du Bois Institute and my hosts, Professors Henry Louis Gates Jr., and Lawrence D. Bobo, for the invitation to give the lectures. And I am grateful to Harvard University Press and its staff, particularly Joyce Seltzer for her prodding, patience, and encouragement, and Maria Louise Ascher, for her careful and thorough editing, corrections, and suggestions.

During the various stages of preparing these lectures, even as I was also completing research for the next book, *Pearl Harbor Blues: The Black South and Race Relations in World War II* (a preview of which may be found in the second chapter), I benefited from the work of some diligent and resourceful graduate research students, most prominently Amy Lippert and Felicia Viator, along with Buzzy Jackson, Bill Wagner, Chris Agee, Kevin Adams, Heather McCarty, and Sam Tepperman-Gelfant. The invaluable assistance these students provided, as well as many of the resource materials, was made possible by the Alexander F. and May T. Morrison Chair in American History at Berkeley.

This book is dedicated to my mentor and friend, Kenneth M. Stampp. In my undergraduate years at Berkeley, he nourished and encouraged my interest in the history of African Americans and race relations. What he taught in his courses would soon materialize in books that changed the ways we thought about slavery and Reconstsruction. As a mentor in graduate school, and as a friend and colleague for nearly half a century, he inspired me by his example as both scholar and teacher.

Rhoda, who knew Nat almost as long as I did, shared my appreciation of his extraordinary qualities. We enjoyed the times spent with Nat and Brenda, in Berkeley, Cambridge, New York, and Paris. Rhoda has heard these lectures more than once and encouraged me as I prepared them for publication. Her support included the love, dedication, and joy she continues to bring to our lives.

Index